An Essay on Demonology, Ghosts and Apparitions, and Popular Superstitions

also, An Account of the Witchcraft Delusion at Salem, in 1682

By James Thacher, M. D., A. A. S.

This Edition Edited by Anthony Uyl

Ingersoll, Ontario, Canada 2025

An Essay on Demonology, Ghosts and Apparitions, and Popular Superstitions

An Essay on Demonology, Ghosts and Apparitions, and Popular Superstitions
also, An Account of the Witchcraft Delusion at Salem, in 1682
By James Thacher, M. D., A. A. S.
This Edition Edited by Anthony Uyl

Originally Published by:
Boston: Carter and Hendee. MDCCC XXXI, 1831

Originally Printed by:
Boston Classic Press. I. R. Butts.

The text of *An Essay on Demonology, Ghosts and Apparitions, and Popular Superstitions: also, An Account of the Witchcraft Delusion at Salem, in 1682* is all protected under Copyright ©2025 Devoted Publishing. The covers, background, layout and Devoted Publishing logo are Copyright ©2025 Devoted Publishing. This edition is published by Devoted Publishing a division of 2165467 Ontario Inc.

Contact us at: devotedpub@hotmail.com
Visit us on X (Formerly Twitter): @AnthonyDevPub

Published in Ingersoll, Ontario, Canada 2025

ISBN: 978-1-77356-551-4

James Thacher, M. D., A. A. S.

Table of Contents

ADVERTISEMENT 5
ESSAY, GHOSTS AND APPARITIONS 6
POWER OF IMAGINATION 11
ILLUSIONS 12
IMAGINATION AND FEAR 17
SUPERSTITION 21
WITCHCRAFT AND SORCERY 24
SALEM WITCHCRAFT 32
    Footnotes: 44
    TRIAL OF SUSANNA MARTIN, JUNE 29, 1692. 44
    TRIAL OF ELIZABETH HOW, JUNE 30, 1692. 45
    TRIAL OF MARTHA CARRYER, AUGUST 2, 1692. 46
OMENS AND AUGURIES 51
MEDICAL QUACKERY 56

'With spells and charms I break the viper's jaw,
Cleave solid rocks, oaks from their fissures draw,
Whole woods remove, the airy mountains shake,
Earth forced to groan, and ghosts from graves awake.'
    - Ovid's Metamor.

There are mysteries even in nature, which we cannot investigate, paradoxes which we can never resolve.

James Thacher, M. D., A. A. S.

ADVERTISEMENT

The following pages were in substance composed to be read before the Plymouth Lyceum, in 1829. When it was understood that Rev. CHARLES W. UPHAM was about to favor the public with a work on the same subject, it was determined that this little performance should be suppressed. The Rev. Author observed in a letter, 'that although we may traverse the same field, it is highly probable that we pursue different tracks. The subject is so various, ample and abundant in instruction, that good rather than evil would result from the application of more than one mind to its discussion.' Since therefore, in the deeply interesting work referred to, the learned author has not particularly discussed the subjects of Ghosts, Apparitions, Mental Illusions, &c, there may be no impropriety in submitting the following imperfect production to the public, with the hope that it will not be considered as altogether superfluous.
    J. T.
    Plymouth, Nov. 1831.

ESSAY, GHOSTS AND APPARITIONS

Such is the constitution of the human mind, that it never attains to perfection; it is constantly susceptible of erroneous impressions and perverse propensities. The faculties of the soul are bound in thraldom by superstition, and the intellect, under its influence, is scarcely capable of reflecting on its divine origin, its nobleness and dignity. The mind that is imbued with a superstitious temperament, is liable to incessant torment, and is prepared to inflict the most atrocious evils on mankind; even murder, suicide, and merciless persecution, have proceeded from, and been sanctioned by a superstitious spirit. It is this, in its most appalling aspect, which impels the heathen to a life of mutilation and perpetual pain and torment of body, which degrades the understanding below that of a brute. The superstitions practised by the devotees to the Roman Catholic Church, if less horrible, are equally preposterous and pernicious. The popular belief in supernatural visitations in the form of apparitions and spectres, is fostered and encouraged by the baneful influence of superstition and prejudice. So universal has been the prevalence of the belief that those conversant with history can resort to the era when every village had its ghost or witch, as, in more ancient times, every family had its household gods. Superstition, is a word of very extensive signification, but for the purpose of this work, the word applies to those who believe in witchcraft, magic, and apparitions, or that the divine will is decided by omens or auguries; that the fortune of individuals can be affected by things indifferent, by things deemed lucky or unlucky, or that disease can be cured by words, charms, and incantations. It means, in short, the belief of what is false and contrary to reason. Superstition arises from, and is sustained by ignorance and credulity in the understanding. The subject of supernatural agency and the reality of witchcraft, has been the occasion of unbounded speculation, and of much philosophical disquisition, in almost all nations and ages. While some of the wisest of men have assented to their actual existence and visible appearance, others equally eminent have maintained the opinion that the supposed apparitions are to be accounted for on the principle of feverish dreams and disturbed imaginations. That our Creator has power to employ celestial spirits as instruments and messengers, and to create supernatural visions on the human mind, it would be impious to deny. But we can conceive of no necessity, at the present day, for the employment of disembodied spirits in our world; we can hold no intercourse with them, nor realize the slightest advantage by their agency. To believe in apparitions is to believe that God suspends the law of nature for the most trivial purposes, and that he would communicate the power of doing mischief, and of controling his laws to beings, merely to gratify their own passions, which is inconsistent with the goodness of God. We are sufficiently aware that the sacred spirits of our fathers have ascended to regions prepared for their reception, and there may they remain undisturbed till the mighty secrets now concealed shall be revealed for our good. The soul or spirit of man is immaterial, of course intangible and invisible. If it is not recognisable by our senses, how can the dead appear to the living? That disembodied spirits should communicate with surviving objects on earth, that the ghosts of the murdered should appear to disclose the murderer, or that the spirit of the wise and good should return to proffer instructions to the vile and ignorant, must be deemed unphilosophical.

It will now be attempted to demonstrate, that the generality of the supposed apparitions, in modern times, will admit of explanation from causes purely natural. For this purpose, it will be requisite first, to describe the system of nerves, and their functions, which constitute a part of our complicated frames. Nerves are to be considered as a tissue of strings or cords, which have their origin in the brain and spinal marrow, and are distributed in branches to all parts of the body. They are the immediate organs of sensation and of muscular action. Upon the integrity of the nerves, all the senses, both external and internal, entirely depend. The nerves are the medium of illusions; their influence pervades the whole body, and their various impressions are transmitted to the brain. When the entire brain is affected, delirium is the consequence; if the optic nerve only, visions disturb the imagination; if the acoustic nerves receive the impression, unreal sounds or voices are heard. If the optic nerves are cut or rendered paralytic, the sense of vision is irrecoverably destroyed. The nervous system is liable to be diseased and deranged from various causes, from which, it is obvious, derangement of both body and mind must ensue. The following is extracted from a lecture on Moral Philosophy, by the learned and Reverend Samuel Stanhope Smith, D. D.,

James Thacher, M. D., A. A. S.
late President of the College of New Jersey.

'The nerves are easily excited into movement by an infinite variety of external impulses, or internal agitations. By whatever impulse any motion, vibration, or affection, in the nervous system is produced, a correspondent sensation, or train of sensations, or ideas in the mind, will naturally follow. When the body is in regular health, and the operations of the mind are in a natural and healthful train, the action of the nervous system, being affected only by the regular and successive impressions made upon it by the objects of nature, as they successively occur, will present to the mind just and true images of the scenes that surround it. But by various species of infirmity and disorder in the body, the nerves, sometimes in their entire system, and sometimes only in those divisions of them which are attached to particular organs of sense, may be subjected to very irregular motions or vibrations. Hence unreal images may be raised in the mind. The state of the nervous affections may be vitiated by intemperate indulgence, or by infirmity resulting from sedentary and melancholy habits. Superstitions, fancies, or enthusiastic emotions, do often greatly disturb the regular action of the nervous system. Such elastic and vibratory strings may be subject to an infinite variety of irregular movements, sometimes in consequence of a disordered state of health, and sometimes arising from peculiarity of constitutional structure, which may present false and often fantastic images to the mind. No cause, perhaps, produces a more anomalous oscitancy, or vibration of the nervous system, or of some particular portions of it, than habits of intemperate indulgence. And I have not unfrequently become acquainted with men who had been addicted to such excesses, who were troubled with apprehensions of supernatural apparitions. A peculiar imbecility of constitution, however, created by study, retirement, or other causes, may be productive of similar effects, and sometimes these nervous anomalies are formed in men who are otherwise of active and athletic constitutions. But where they possess enlightened minds and vigorous understandings, such visionary tendencies may be counteracted by their intellectual energies. Yet have we sometimes known the strongest understandings overcome by the vivacity of nervous impression, which frequently is scarcely inferior to the most lively ideas of sense. This may, especially, be the case in two opposite conditions: either when the body has fallen into a gloomy temperament, and the mind is weakened by fears, in which case it is oppressed by distressing apprehensions; or, on the other hand, when the nerves, the primary organs, of sensation, are strained into an unnatural tension, and the whole system is exalted by an enthusiastic fervor to the pitch of delirious intoxication. When a man is exalted to such a degree of nervous excitement and mental feeling, his visions are commonly pleasing, often rapturous, and sometimes fantastic; but generally rise above the control or correction of the judgment. Lord Lyttleton, in the vision which he believed he saw of his deceased mother's form, shortly before his own death, may be an example of the former; and the Baron Von Swedenborg, in his supposed visions, sometimes of angels and sometimes of reptiles, may be an instance of the latter. Persons, whose fancies have been much disturbed in early life, by the tales of nurses, and other follies of an injudicious education, creating a timid and superstitious mind, are more especially liable to have their fears alarmed and their imagination excited by every object in the dark. Whence sounds will be augmented to the ear, and images rendered more glaring to the eyes.'

In a note, the learned author presents the following examples, tending to illustrate the principles just advanced.

'I knew, some years ago, a worthy lady who, anxiously watching by the cradle of a sick infant, and momently expecting its death, felt, as she believed, just before it expired, a violent stroke across the back of both her arms. From a tincture of superstitious apprehension infused in her early education, and unacquainted with any natural cause of such a phenomenon, she construed it into a preternatural signal of the death of her child. It was, probably, a sudden and convulsive contraction of the muscles in that part of the system, occasioned by the solicitude of her mind and the fatigue of watching, which, aided by imagination in a very interesting moment, produced a shock that had to her the feeling of a severe concussion. That a convulsive contraction should take place in those particular muscles need not appear strange to those who know how irregular and uncertain is the whole train of nervous action, especially under the operation of some disorders of the body; and frequently, under the influence of strong affections and emotions of the mind.' 'A young lady, who was peculiarly susceptible of the impressions of fear in the dark, or at the sight of any of the accompaniments of death, attended the funeral of one of her intimate companions, who had died of the small pox. On the following night she lodged in company with a female friend of great firmness of mind. Waking in the night, some time after the moon had risen, and faintly enlightened her chamber, the first object that struck her view was a white robe hanging on the tall back of a chair, and a cap placed on the top. Her disturbed imagination instantly took the alarm, and in her agitation and terror rousing her companion, she exclaimed violently that her deceased friend was standing before her. The lady, with great presence of mind, brought the articles of clothing which had caused the alarm, and thus composed her fears. After she had become tranquil and was able distinctly to recall her sensations, she declared that the perfect image of the deceased, just as she was dressed for her coffin seemed to be before her sight. She contemplated it as long as her fears would permit her, before she exclaimed. She was sure that she recognised every feature of her friend, and even the pits of the small pox, of which she died, in her face. And she affirmed that before any tribunal she would have been willing to make oath to this fact.' 'I have introduced this anecdote,' says Dr Smith, 'merely to illustrate the power of the imagination by its reaction on the nervous system, to complete the pictures that any sudden impulses of the senses, occasioned by surprise or by superstitious or enthusiastic feeling, have begun to form. It is not a solitary anecdote of the kind. But I have selected it, because I am more perfectly possessed of the circumstances, than of many others that are circulated through certain classes of society. Nor are these classes always to be found among the most ignorant and credulous.' Lord Lyttleton was a man of splendid abilities, but degraded himself by a continued course of profligacy and the basest dissipation. He was arrested in his career by a sudden and remarkable death, at the age of thirtyfive in the year 1779. The various narrations that have been published relative to this singular event concur in most of the following particulars. Three days previous to his death, being in perfect health, he was warned in a dream or vision of the event, which, accordingly, took place without any previous illness. According to his own account, he awoke from sleep, and saw the image of his deceased mother, who opened the curtains of his bed and denounced to him, that in three days he should die. On the sentence being denounced, he started up in great terror, incoherently saying, 'what! shall I not live three days?' The reply was, no, you will not live more than three days, and the apparition instantly vanished. This alarming vision his lordship related, at breakfast the next morning, to several women who were his companions. They fell a crying; but he, although secretly agitated, pretended to disregard the affair, laughed at their credulous folly, and professed to have no sort of belief, or apprehension about it. On the third day of the prediction, he invited Admiral Woolsey and another friend to dine with him, at his country seat. At dinner, his lordship, appeared more than usually loquacious and desultory in his conversation, reciting the probable remarks that would of course be made whenever the news of his death should be announced. In the evening, perceiving his female companions in a gloomy mood, he took one of them and danced a minuet with her, then taking out his watch, said, 'Look you here, it is now nine o'clock, according to the vision I have but three hours to live, but don't you mind this, madam; never fear, we'll jocky the ghost, I warrant you.' At eleven o'clock he retired to bed earlier than usual with him, but his pretence was, that he had planned for the party to breakfast early, and spend the day in riding into the country. Admiral Woolsey and his friend resolved to sit in the parlor till the predicted hour was past, and the clock was privately put a little forward, and as soon as it struck twelve, his lordship said, 'you see I have cheated the ghost;' but soon after a voice was heard from the staircase, uttering these words. 'He's dead? Oh, my lord is dead!' Instantly running up stairs, they found him in bed, fallen back, and struggling. Admiral Woolsey took his hand, which was grasped with such violence that it was painful to endure, but he spake no more. His eyes were turned up and fixed. They opened the jugular vein, but no blood issued, and he was entirely dead at midnight of the third day. Admiral Woolsey gives the following remarkable particulars in addition. At the distance of thirty miles from the place where this melancholy scene happened there lived a gentlemen, one of the intimate companions of Lord Lyttleton, M. P. Andrews, Esq.; and they had agreed that whichever of them should die first, the survivor should receive one thousand pounds from the estate of the deceased. On this very night he awoke about one o'clock and rung his bell with great violence. His servant ran to him with all speed, and inquired, 'what is the matter?' The gentleman sitting up in bed, with a countenance full of horror, cried out, 'Oh John! Lord Lyttleton is dead!' 'How can that be?' he replied, 'we have heard nothing, but that he is alive and well.' The master exclaimed with the greatest perturbation, 'no, no, I awoke just now on hearing the curtains undrawn, and at the foot of the bed stood Lord Lyttleton, as plain as ever I saw him in my life. He looked ghastly, and said, "all is over with me, Andrews. You have won the thousand pounds," and vanished.' After attending to the particulars above detailed, it would seem to require a philosophical firmness to resist the impression in favor of supernatural visitations; but this latter instance will, I believe, bear a different explanation. The gentleman was apprised of Lyttleton's vision and predicted death, which, with the thousand pounds depending, must have excited in his mind an exquisite degree of anxiety, and roused a guilty conscience. He doubtless counted every hour, and although he fell asleep, could not be calm, and probably had a disturbed dream. Awaking suddenly, it is quite natural that he should have the impression, that the prediction was fulfilled. Dr Smith, who is quoted above, comments as follows on the death of Lord Lyttleton. His lordship was a man who had worn down to a very feeble state, a lively and elastic constitution, and impaired a brilliant wit, by voluptuous, and intemperate excesses. A few days before his death, he imagined that he saw before him the perfect resemblance of his deceased mother, who denounced to him that on such a day, and at a prescribed hour, he should die. Under a constrained vivacity, his mind, during the interval, was evidently much agitated. And on the predicted day, and at the prescribed time, he actually expired.

This fact has been regarded by many persons, and those by no means of inferior understandings, as a decisive proof of the reality of apparitions from the spiritual world; and by others has been attempted to be resolved on a variety of different grounds. The principles already suggested, may, perhaps, serve to explain it in conformity with the known laws of human nature, if the theory of nervous vibration be admitted to be true, without resorting to the solution of supernatural agents. The irregular and convulsive motions in the nervous system which frequently arise from long continued habits of intemperate indulgence, might be especially expected in a constitution so irritable and debilitated, as that of Lord Lyttleton. If, either sleeping or waking, or, in that indefinite interval between sleeping and waking, their disordered movements could present to the fancy or excite in the visual nerves, the distinct image of a living person apparently resuscitated from the dead, which has been shown to be a possible case, the debilitated frame of his lordship, agitated as it must have often been, by the conscious apprehension of his approaching end, may naturally be supposed to have predisposed them to such a vision. Conscience, notwithstanding his assumed gayety, somewhat perturbed by the fears of death, and with a recollection of a pious mother, whose anxious admonitions had often endeavored in vain to recall him from his vices, and to fix his thoughts on his future existence, might naturally retrace her features in this formidable vision. It is not improbable, that the whole scene may have been a kind of waking dream, or if it was wholly transacted in sleep, it might have been with such a forcible and vivid vibration, or impulse of the nerves concerned in the formation of such an image, as would give it the distinctness and vivacity of waking sensation. In the tumult of his spirits, and the fear-excited vibrations of his whole system, it is not strange, that the image of that disappointed and reproaching parent should be presented to him, with a solemn and foreboding aspect. And it would be adding only one trait of terror to the scene, already so well prepared to admit it, and one that is perfectly conformable to our experience of the desultory images of dreaming, as well as what we have learned of similar visionary impressions--that a particular period should be denounced to him for his death, the symptoms and presages of which, in all probability, he frequently felt in the tremors and palpitation of a breaking constitution. The principal difficulty in the minds of those who have only carelessly attended to this history, is to account for the exact correspondence of the event of his death to the time fixed by the prediction, if it had no other foundation than nervous impression. The imagined prediction itself was sufficient, in a debilitated and exhausted constitution, like that of Lord Lyttleton, to produce its own accomplishment. Seizing upon his fears, in spite of his reason and philosophy, for a life of dissipation and sensual excess generally very much weakens the powers both of the mind and of the body, it would naturally throw his whole system into great commotion. These perturbed and tumultuous agitations would increase as the destined moment approached, till the strength of nature failing, may well be supposed to break at the point of extreme convulsion; that is, at the expected moment of death.

To a case analogous, in many respects, to that of his lordship, there are many witnesses still living in the city of Philadelphia. The contrast in the issue of the latter, serves to confirm the solution which has just been given of the former. Mr Edwards, a clergyman of the Baptist persuasion in that city, of a tendency somewhat addicted to melancholy in his habit, but, otherwise of a vigorous constitution, had, like Lord Lyttleton, a visual impression, so clear and distinctly defined, that he mistook it for a supernatural messenger from the spiritual world to announce to him that at the end of a certain period, he should die. He was so persuaded of the reality of the vision, and the verity of the prediction, that he took leave of his particular friends, and of his congregation, before the appointed day. On the evening of this day, I saw his house filled with spectators and inquirers, awaiting with solicitude the catastrophe of this extraordinary affair. The tumult of his whole system, his difficult respiration, his quick and tremulous pulse, and its frequent intermissions, led many to announce, at various times during that evening, to the surrounding spectators, that he was just expiring. And without doubt, if his frame had been as weak and delicate as his nervous system, he could not have survived the agitations, and, I may say, almost convulsions, into which he was thrown. And here would have been another prediction, and another supernatural appearance, as extraordinary as those of Lord Lyttleton. But his constitution triumphed, and he remained a monument to prove the force of nervous illusion, which, in this case, as doubtless it has proved in many others, appears to have given birth to an image as clear and definite as could have been produced by the actual presence of such an object as was supposed to have created it. I would hardly have ventured to relate such an anecdote, if there were not ample testimony to its verity still existing. The good man was so ashamed of his delusion, and it so much lessened his credit with his spiritual flock, that he was obliged to leave the city, and the church where he had formerly been highly esteemed, and retire to a remote position in the country. Many anecdotes to confirm the reality of nervous sensation, if I may apply that phrase to designate those sensible perceptions which are sometimes caused in the mind, without the presence or aid of external objects, must have occurred to those who have had extensive opportunities of practically observing human nature. With several persons I have been acquainted, and those by no means of inferior understanding, who have been firmly persuaded of the existence of the spectres indicated by such nervous affections, and have, on such occasions, held conversations with them, real on their part, imaginary on the part of the supposed spectre. Such, perhaps, in general, are the disciples of the Baron Von Swedenborg. But illusions of this nature are not confined to this class of men alone.

James Thacher, M. D., A. A. S.

POWER OF IMAGINATION

Dr Van Cleve, of Princeton, was lately applied to as a physician on behalf of a man who had reduced himself by intemperance, to a state of very distressing nervous irregularity. He was continually disturbed by visions, sometimes of the most fantastic kind. He often heard strange voices, and would ask and answer questions, as if engaged in conversation with some of his visionary personages. His disorder, the doctor said, was evidently not of that species which is usually denominated mania, but appeared to be wholly the effect of a habit of nervous irregularity, delirium tremens, induced by previous intemperance. But the Baron Von Swedenborg, in his most visionary moments, was never surrounded by more extraordinary assemblages of strange sights. A very striking example of the power of nervous impression, occurred a few years ago in the Rev. James Wilson, formerly assistant minister with Dr Rodgers, in the first Presbyterian Church in New York. He was a native of Scotland, and was a man highly esteemed for his good sense, and the soundness of his judgment; although not distinguished for a warm and popular eloquence. Being obliged for a time to relinquish the exercise of his ministry from a hemorrhage in his breast, he employed himself for several years in different occupations in Scotland and America, but chiefly in presiding over an Academy in Alexandria, in the State of Virginia. The expectoration of blood having ceased for a considerable time, his conscience began to reproach him for indolence and self-indulgence, in not renewing his ministerial functions. In this uneasy state of mind, a vision, as he thought, of a man of very dignified aspect, stood at the foot of his bed in the morning, after he was perfectly awake, and surveying him steadily for some moments, commanded him to resume his duties in the pulpit: but added, that as considerable error had crept into the church, he should undertake to reform it according to the model of the primitive age. Mr Wilson, conscious of his want of eloquent talents, and reforming zeal, reasoned with the supposed apparition, alleging his utter incompetency to the task imposed upon him. The dialogue ended in a repetition of the command, and assurance of ability and success. The good man, wholly unable to explain this clear and palpable vision, on any principles of nature or philosophy with which he was acquainted, was deeply distressed, yet perfectly sensible of his insufficiency for such an undertaking, he neglected attempting to fulfil it. After an interval of two or three years, the vision was repeated, with nearly the same circumstances, except that the aspect of the person who appeared to present himself, was more severe, and expressive of displeasure at his past delinquency. Mr Wilson repeated his former reasonings on his want of health, and want of talents, with other topics. But the answer was still the same; a repetition of the injunction, and assurance of the necessary ability, and ultimate success. His distress was raised to the highest degree in the conflict of his mind between what he thought a sensible demonstration of a supernatural requisition, and an invincible consciousness of his own incompetency, and his fear of doing an injury to true religion by his failure. After consulting several of his friends upon the subject, he at length addressed a letter to the author, stating all the circumstances which have just been detailed. He was answered with the general reasonings contained in this lecture, to convince him that his vision was merely a consequence of nervous affection, resulting from bodily disorder. Three letters passed between Mr Wilson and the author, reasoned on the part of Mr Wilson with great calmness and good sense, admitting all the objections to such an apostolic undertaking as that to which he was urged, both from scripture and from his own peculiar deficiency of power and talents, but pleading the impulse of a sensation as clear and strong, and, to his mind, as real as he had ever felt. But it was replied that there were other considerations combined with the whole system and harmony of nature, which ought to have greater authority with a rational mind than any single and individual impression of sense, which evidently violates its general order. The correspondence came to this issue at last, that, as he agreed with the church as she now exists, in most of her doctrines, and especially in the moral precepts of religion, he should begin his course by inculcating only those principles in which all were agreed, and if he found the promise of his vision verified in his returning strength and successful eloquence, he would then have sufficient encouragement to proceed further. He actually came to New York with the intention to put this experiment into execution, but died in that city shortly after his landing. He published one discourse introductory to the design.

ILLUSIONS

The following observations are from Dr Rush, found in his Treatise on Diseases of the Mind. 'By this term, (Illusions) I mean that disease, in which false perceptions take place in the ears and eyes in the waking state, from a morbid affection of the brain, or of the sense which is the seat of the illusion. It may be considered as a waking dream. Persons affected with it fancy they hear voices, or see objects that do not exist. These false perceptions are said, by superstitious people, to be premonitions of death. They sometimes indicate either the forming state, or the actual existence of disease, which being seated most commonly in a highly vital part of the body, that is, in the brain, now and then ends in death, and thus administers support to superstition. They depend, like false perception in madness, upon motion being excited in a part of the ear or the eye, which does not vibrate with the impression made upon it, but communicates it to a part upon which the impression of the noise heard, or of the person seen, was formerly made, and hence the one becomes audible, and the other visible.

'The deception, when made upon the ears, consists most commonly in hearing our own names, and for this obvious reason; we are accustomed to hear them pronounced more frequently than any other words, and hence the part of the ear, which vibrates with the sound of our names, moves more promptly, from habit, than any other part of it. For the same reason the deception, when made upon the eyes, consists in seeing our own persons, or the persons of our intimate friends, whether living or dead, oftener than any other people. The part upon the retina, from which those images are reflected, move more promptly, from habit, than any other of that part of the organ of vision.

'The voice which is supposed to be heard, and the objects which are supposed to be seen, are never heard nor seen by two persons, even when they are close to each other. This proves them both to be the effect of disease in the single person who hears, or sees, the supposed voice or object.'

Dr Rush has recorded numerous instances of partial mental derangement from hypochondriasis, chiefly from his own knowledge, such as the following. A sea captain believed that he had a wolf in his liver; others that they are converted into an animal of another species, such as a goose, a dog, a cat, a hare, a cow, and the like. One imagined that he was once a calf, and mentions the name of the butcher that killed him, and the stall in the Philadelphia market, on which his flesh was sold, previously to his animating his present body. One believed that he had no soul. Another that he is transformed into a plant, and insisted on being watered in common with all the plants around him in the garden. Another that his body was transformed into glass. The celebrated Cowper suffered much anguish from complaints of a similar nature, arising from hypochondriac affection.

Among the causes of nervous affection and diseased imagination, are those of sedentary habits and a free use of strong tea. The following instances were communicated by my friend the Rev. Mr K.

The late Rev. Mr F. of Ipswich, who was very sedentary; spent most of his time in his study without exercise, and his health became impaired. He imagined for some time before his death, that he was actually dead. I saw him in this state of mind, walking his chamber in extreme agitation. To the question, how he could suffer so much, if actually dead, he answered, that his own spirit was departed, and that another spirit had taken possession of his body.

A gentleman in Boston once told the first President Adams, that he had become strangely timid, that he dared not keep the side walks, but walked in the middle of the street, being constantly apprehensive that the tile on the houses would fall on his head. The president asked him if he made a free use of tea, and being answered in the affirmative, he recommended to him to use it more sparingly and he would probably be benefited by the change. By pursuing this advice, he was relieved, and was soon able to return to the side walks without fear.

A gentleman of Salem, sailing from the south to Massachusetts, while under the influence of nervous affection, imagined that he saw a man in the water near the ship, who was drowning. Conceiving that he might save his life, he was in the very act of leaping into the sea for that purpose, but was happily prevented by those on deck. He afterward recovered his health, and had a perfect recollection of his feelings on that occasion. He had no idea of destroying himself, but would have perished had he not been prevented. Instances of a similar nature have probably occurred, in which lives have been lost in consequence of such delusion.

It is said that Mr Murdock, the member of the Vermont Legislature, who recently committed suicide, imagined himself to be Dr Cleaveland, who was under sentence of death. Mr Murdock attempted to speak when Cleaveland's case was before the legislature, but was so much agitated that he could not speak, and was taken from the house by his friends. Under this strong impression of his being Cleaveland, he killed himself to avoid the doom of the law. This event would make a thrilling chapter in Sir Walter Scott's history of Demonology and Witchcraft.

It will aid our purpose to relate the following instance of Mr Nicolai, an intelligent bookseller and member of the Academy of Sciences of Berlin, who happily possessed philosophy enough to account for the phantasms which, for some time agitated his own mind, upon rational principles. 'In the year 1791, I was much affected in my mind by several incidents of a very disagreeable nature; and on a certain day a circumstance occurred, which irritated me extremely. At ten o'clock in the forenoon, my wife and another person came to console me. I was in a violent perturbation of mind, owing to a series of incidents which had altogether wounded my moral feelings, and from which I saw no possibility of relief; when suddenly I observed at the distance of ten paces from me, a figure; the figure of a deceased person. I pointed at it, and asked my wife if she did not see it. She saw nothing; but being much alarmed, endeavored to compose me, and sent for the physician. The figure remained seven or eight minutes, and at length I became a little more calm; and as I was extremely exhausted, I soon afterwards fell into a troubled kind of slumber, which lasted for half an hour. The vision was ascribed to the great agitation of mind in which I had been, and it was supposed I should have nothing more to apprehend from that cause; but the violent affection had put my nerves into some unnatural state; from this arose further consequences which require a more detailed description. In the afternoon a little after four o'clock, the figure which I had seen in the morning again appeared. I was alone when this happened, a circumstance, which, as may easily be conceived, could not be very agreeable. I went therefore to the apartment of my wife, to whom I related it. But thither also the figure pursued me. Sometimes it was present, sometimes it vanished, but it was always the same standing figure. A little after six o'clock, several stalking figures also appeared, but they had no connexion with the standing figure. The figure of the deceased person never appeared to me after the first dreadful day; but several other figures showed themselves afterwards very distinctly; sometimes such as I knew, mostly however, of persons I did not know, and amongst those known to me, were the semblance of both living and deceased persons, but mostly the former; and I made the observation, that acquaintance with whom I daily conversed never appeared to me as phantasms; it was always such as were at a distance. These figures appeared to me at all times, and under the most different circumstances, equally distinct and clear. Whether I was alone or in company, by broad day light equally as in the night time, in my own house as well as in my neighbor's; yet, when I was at another person's house, they were less frequent, and when I walked the public street, they very seldom appeared. When I shut my eyes, sometimes the figures disappeared, sometimes they remained even after I closed them. If they vanished in the former case, on opening my eyes again, nearly the same figures appeared which I had seen before. For the most part I saw human figures of both sexes; they commonly passed to and fro, as if they had no connexion with each other, like people at a fair, where all is bustle; sometimes they appeared to have business with each other. Once or twice I saw amongst them persons on horseback, and dogs and birds; these figures all appeared to me in their natural size, as distinctly as if they had existed in real life, with the several tints on the uncovered parts of the body, and with all the different kinds and colors of clothes. On the whole, the longer I continued in this state, the more did the phantasms increase, and the apparitions became more frequent. About four weeks afterwards, I began to hear them speak, sometimes the phantasms spoke with one another; but for the most part they addressed themselves to me; these speeches were in general short, and never contained anything disagreeable. Intelligent and respected friends often appeared to me, who endeavored to console me in my grief, which still left deep traces on my mind. This speaking I heard most frequently when I was alone; though I sometimes heard it in company, intermingled with the conversation of real persons, frequently in single phrases only, but sometimes even in connected discourse. Though at this time I enjoyed rather a good state of health both in body and mind, and had become so familiar with these phantasms, that at last they did not excite the least disagreeable emotion, but on the contrary afforded me frequent subjects for amusement and mirth; yet as the disorder sensibly increased, and the figures appeared to me the whole day together, and even during the night, if I happened to awake, I had recourse to several medicines. Had I not been able to distinguish phantasms from phenomena, I must have been insane. Had I been fanatic or superstitious, I should have been terrified at my own phantasms, and probably might have been seized with some alarming disorder. Had I been attached to the marvellous, I should have sought to magnify my own importance, by asserting that I had seen spirits; and who could have disputed the facts with me? In this case, however, the advantage of sound philosophy and deliberate observation may be seen. Both prevented me from becoming either a lunatic or an enthusiast; for with nerves so strongly excited, and blood so quick in circulation, either misfortune might have easily befallen me. But I considered the phantasms that hovered around me as what they really were, namely, the effects of disease, and made them subservient to my observations, because I consider observation and reflection as the basis of all rational philosophy.' This gentleman had been accustomed to lose blood twice a year, but it was omitted at this time, and having suffered so much by the neglect, he again had recourse to blood letting and was soon relieved of all his phantasms.

The following article is contained in the Edinburgh Journal of Science, conducted by Dr Brewster, who says of the narrator of the case, that, 'his station in society and as a man of science, would authenticate the minutest particulars in his narrative, and satisfy the most scrupulous reader that the case has been philosophically as well as faithfully described.' The narrator is in fact the husband of the lady who was the subject of the disease.

'On the twentysixth of December, 1829, about half past four o'clock in the afternoon, Mrs B. was standing near the fire in the hall, and on the point of going up stairs to dress, when she heard, as she supposed, my voice calling her by name,--Come here, come to me! She imagined that I was calling at the door to have it opened, went to it, and was surprised on opening it to find no one. She returned toward the fire, and again heard the same voice, calling very distinctly and loud,--Come, come here. She then opened two other doors of the same room, but seeing no one, she returned to the fire-place. After a few minutes, she heard the same voice, still calling--'Come to me, come, come away;' this time in a loud, plaintive, and somewhat impatient tone. She answered as loudly--'Where are you? I don't know where you are'--still imagining that I was somewhere in search of her; but receiving no answer, she shortly went up stairs. On my return to the house about half an hour afterwards, she inquired why I had called to her so often, and where I was; and was of course surprised to hear I had not been near the house at the time.

'On the 30th of the same month, at about four o'clock, P. M., Mrs B. came down stairs into the drawing room, which she had quitted a few minutes before, and on entering the room, saw me, as she supposed, standing with my back to the fire. She addressed me, asking how it was I had returned so soon. (I had left the house for a walk half an hour before.) She said I looked fixedly at her with a serious and thoughtful expression of countenance, but did not speak. She supposed I was busied in thought, and sat down in an arm-chair near the fire, and within a couple of feet at most of the figure she still saw standing before her. As, however, the eyes still continued to be fixed upon her, after a few moments she said--'Why don't you speak--?' The figure upon this moved off towards the window at the farther end of the room, the eyes still gazing on her, and passed so very close to her in doing so, that she was struck by the circumstance of hearing no step nor sound, nor feeling her clothes brushed against, nor even any agitation of the air. The idea then arose for the first time into her mind, that it was no reality, but a spectral illusion, (being a person of sense and habituated to account rationally for most things, the notion of anything supernatural was out of the question.) She recollected, however, your having mentioned that there was a sort of experimentum crucis, applicable to these cases, by which a genuine ghost may be distinguished from one conjured up by merely natural causes; namely, the pressing the eye in order to produce the effect of seeing double, when, according to your assertion, a true Tartarean ghost may be duplicated as well as everything else; while the morbid idea being, I suppose, an impression on the retina, would or ought to remain single. I am sorry, however, to say, that the opportunity for verifying your theory was unfavorable. Before Mrs B. was able distinctly to double her vision, my figure had retreated to the window and disappeared there. The lady followed, shook the curtains, and tried the windows, being still loth to believe it was not a reality, so distinct and forcible was the impression. Finding, however, that there was no natural means of egress, she became convinced of having seen a spectral apparition, such as are recorded in Dr Hibbert's work, and consequently felt no alarm or agitation. The appearance lasted four or five minutes. It was bright daylight, and Mrs B. is confident that the apparition was fully as vivid as the reality; and when standing close to her, it concealed, of course, the real objects behind it. Upon being told of this my visible appearance in the spirit, having been only audible a few days before, I was, as you may imagine, more alarmed for the health of the lady than for my own approaching death, or any other fatality the vision might be supposed to forebode. Still both the stories were so very much en regle as ghost stories, the three calls of the plaintive voice, each one louder than the preceding, the fixed eye and mournful expression of the phantom, its noiseless step and spirit-like vanishing, were all so characteristic of the wraith, that I might have been unable to shake off some disagreeable fancies, such as a mind once deeply saturated with the poison of nursery-tales cannot altogether banish, had it not been for a third apparition, at whose visit I myself assisted, a few days afterwards, and which I think is the key-stone of the case, rendering it as complete as could be wished.

'On the 4th of this month, January, 1830, five days after the last apparition, at about ten o'clock at night, I was sitting in the drawing-room with Mrs B. and in the act of stirring the fire, when she exclaimed, 'Why, there's the cat in the room!' I asked 'Where?' She replied, 'There, close to you.' 'Where?' I repeated. 'Why, on the rug, to be sure, between yourself and the coal-scuttle.' I had the poker in my hand, and I pushed it in the direction mentioned. 'Take care,' she cried out, 'take care, you are hitting her with the poker.' I again asked her to point out exactly where she saw the cat. She replied, 'Why, sitting up there close to your feet, on the rug:--she is looking at me. It is Kitty, come here Kitty.' There are two cats in the house, one of which went by this name. They are rarely, if ever in the drawing-room. At this time Mrs B. had certainly no idea that the sight of the cat was an illusion. I asked her to touch it. She got up for the purpose, and seemed, too, as if she was pursuing something which moved away. She followed a few steps, and then said,--'It has gone under that chair.' I told her it was an illusion. She would not believe it. I lifted up the chair; there was nothing there, nor did Mrs B. see anything more of it. I searched the room all over, and found nothing. There was a dog lying on the hearth, who would have betrayed great uneasiness had a cat been in the room. He was perfectly quiet. In order to be quite certain, I rung the bell and sent for the cats. They were both found in the housekeeper's room. The most superstitious person could now doubt no longer as to the real character of all these illusory appearances, and the case is so complete, that I hope there will be no renewal of them, symptomatic as they of course are of a disordered state of the body. I am sorry to say Mrs B. as well as myself, forgot to try in time the experimentum crucis on the cat. Mrs B. has naturally a morbidly sensitive imagination, so strongly affecting her corporeal impressions, that the story of any person having severe pain by accident, or otherwise, will occasionally produce acute twinges of pain in the correspondent part in her own person. An account, for instance, of the amputation of an arm, will produce an instantaneous and severe sense of pain in her own arm; and so of other relations. She is subject to talk in her sleep, with great fluency; to repeat poetry very much at length, particularly when unwell, and even cap verses for half an hour together, never failing to quote lines beginning with the final letter of the preceding till her memory is exhausted.

'She has, during the last six weeks, been considerably reduced and weakened, by a tiresome cough, which has also added to her weakness by preventing the taking a daily tonic, to which she had been for some time accustomed. She had also confined herself from this cause to the house for some weeks, which is not usual with her, being accustomed to take a great deal of air and exercise. Her general health for some time past has not been strong, and a long experience has proved beyond a doubt, that her ill health is attributable to a disordered state of the digestive organs. These details are necessary for a complete understanding of this case, which strikes me as one of remarkable interest, from combining the character of an ordinary ghost story with those of an indubitable illusion, as well as from the circumstance occurring to a person of strong mind, devoid of any superstitious fancies, and to be implicitly relied on for the truth of the minutest details of the appearances. Indeed, I do not recollect any well authenticated and recent instances of auricular delusion like the first of those I have related, though of course the warning voices and sounds which have frightened too many weak persons into their graves, must have been of this nature. Mrs B. tells me that about ten years ago a similar circumstance happened to her when residing in Florence, and in perfect health. While undressing after a ball, she heard a voice call her repeatedly by name, and was at that time unable to account for the fact.

'It was nearly a month after the last occurrence, that Mrs B. was preparing for bed at about eleven o'clock at night, and after somewhat a fatiguing day, and sitting before the dressing glass occupied in arranging her hair. She describes her state of mind at the time as listless and drowsy, but fully awake; indeed her fingers were in active motion among the papillotes, when she was suddenly startled by seeing in the mirror the figure of a near relative (at the time in Scotland) over her left shoulder; her eyes meeting his in the glass. The figure was enveloped in grave clothes, closely pinned as is usual with corpses round the head and under the chin. Though the eyes were open, the features were solemn and rigid. The dress was decidedly a shroud, as Mrs B. remarked even the punctured pattern worked in a peculiar manner round the edges of that garment. Mrs B. describes herself as sensible of a feeling like fascination, compelling her for a time to gaze on this melancholy apparition, which was as distinct and vivid as any reflected reality could be; the light of the candles on the dressing table appearing to shine fully upon it. After a few minutes she turned round to look for the reality of the form over her shoulder. It was not, however, visible; and had also disappeared from the glass when she looked in that direction again. Coupled with the previous illusions I related to you, this last apparition becomes more interesting than it would be alone. In the first place, its melancholy and indeed horrible character, distinguishes it from the others, but brings it still nearer the ordinary stories of supernatural visitation. At the same time the possible continuance of such spectral appearances is highly disagreeable, however firm the lady's nerves, and however sound her philosophy. 2d. The mind in this case seems not to have had the remotest influence in raising or dissipating the illusion. Mrs B. is convinced there was no train of thought previously passing through her mind, likely to have the slightest association with the idea of the relative, whose form she suddenly saw with all the distinctness of reality. 3d. The former illusions might be supposed ideas of sensation, sounds, or pictures reproduced, with extraordinary vividness in the same shape and character, in which they had been perceived by and stored up in the mind. But in this last case there is a new combination of ideas which never entered the mind in connexion.

'The union of the well known features with the shroud, must have been a pure effort of, or creation of the mind. There seems, therefore, no reason why, under the same disposition of the nervous system, any monstrous creation of the faculty we call imagination might not be produced to the eyes and other senses; indeed, with all the qualities that constitute reality, except their endurance, though this should hardly be excepted, since there can be no reason why the appearances may not endure, by a continuance of the conditions for days, or months. I need hardly say that the relative, whose ghost was seen after so dismal a fashion, was at the time in perfect health. Had it been otherwise, and the apparition coincided with illness or death, as has no doubt frequently happened in other instances, our philosophy would have had to stand a severe trial.'

James Thacher, M. D., A. A. S.

IMAGINATION AND FEAR

The influence of the imagination on the nervous system has on some occasions produced effects bordering on a state of insanity. It deprives the mind of all correct reasonings, perverts the understanding with which we are endowed by our Creator to regulate our belief, guide us in our pursuits, and enable us to trace effects to their true causes. Instances are not wanting, in which the imagination has been so highly excited as to produce fatal effects. We have on record, among others, the story of a German student, who dreamed he was to die at a certain hour the next day. He immediately made his will, and prepared himself for the awful event. Every argument was used to convince him that no dependence is to be put in dreams, but without shaking his belief, and as the hour approached, he exhibited the alarming signs of death. He watched the clock with the greatest anxiety, till his attending physician contrived to place the hands of the clock beyond the specified hour, when his mind was relieved from the impression, and he was rejoiced to find that he might still continue to live in despite of his dream. In another instance, a man whose nervous system was impaired, and imagination excited, conceived the extravagant idea, that his legs were made of glass, and would use no exercise lest he should break them. He was prevailed on, however, to ride, and the carriage was designedly overset, when he was soon convinced that his legs were made of the substantial material intended by nature. A few years since, Elijah Barns of Pennsylvania, killed a rattlesnake in his field without any injury to himself, and immediately after put on his son's waistcoat, mistaking it for his own, both being of one color. He returned to his house, and on attempting to button his waistcoat, he found to his astonishment that it was much too small. His imagination was now wrought to a high pitch, and he instantly conceived the idea that he had been bitten imperceptibly by the snake, and was thus swollen from its poison. He grew suddenly very ill, and took to his bed. The family in great alarm and confusion summoned three physicians, and the usual remedies were prescribed and administered. The patient, however, grew worse and worse every minute, until at length his son came home with his father's waistcoat dangling about him. The mystery was instantly unfolded, and the patient being relieved from his imaginary apprehensions, dismissed his physicians, and was restored to health.

The philosophy of mind is a study of peculiar interest, and after all our powers of research are exhausted, numerous phenomena will remain inexplicable. Indeed our mental faculties are continually overwhelmed with things inexplicable. We too often embrace for substantial truths mere phantoms, which vanish into air, and leave the mind to deplore its own imbecility. While superstition weakens our moral virtues, and the influence of imagination deludes our intellectual powers, the passion of fear has a pernicious and even a hazardous tendency. It is the passion, which most of all others, exerts its effects directly on the heart; on some occasions, it produces instant death, and in numerous instances, it lays a foundation for a chronic disease of that vital organ, which, after a long duration of distressing complaints, has a fatal termination. Not long since, an instance was published, of a child having died of a disease of the heart, in consequence of a fright received by being thrown upwards and caught in its fall for amusement.

Few persons are aware of the extreme danger of sudden fright on timid minds. The most melancholy consequences have on some occasions resulted from stratagems with effigies, representing apparitions for innocent and momentary amusement. Instances are not wanting of a total loss of intellect during life, from such inexcusable folly. Parents and nurses should carefully avoid imbuing the minds of children with idle stories of ghosts and apparitions. The following facts, selected from numerous others, will illustrate the effects of terror on the mind. In a poorhouse in Haerlem, a girl was seized with a convulsive disorder, which returned in regular paroxysms; not long after, another was taken, and others in succession, till all the boys and girls in the house were affected in a similar manner. The medical prescriptions failed to perform a cure. At length the celebrated Dr Boerhaave, ascribing the occurrences to the habit of imitation, ordered several furnaces to be placed in the chamber. Over the burning coals a number of crooked irons were laid, and the doctor ordered his attendants to burn the arm of the first child, who should be seized in a fit, even to the bone. This alarming remedy produced the desired effect; their imagination was overpowered by the force of fear, and not a case of the kind again occurred. In a family of six children, one of them was afflicted with convulsive affections; all the others exhibited the symptoms of the same disorder, by imitation. No remedy could remove the extraordinary affection, till the father placed a block and an axe in their view, and declared that he would decapitate the first one who should exhibit any more gestures, except the first one taken. By this expedient, all imitation and imaginary feelings were overcome, and the five last were happily delivered from the nervous agitations. With respect to the appearance of ghosts and apparitions, it cannot be doubted, but many of the reports found on record, or repeated by tradition, were mere illusions of imagination, or fictions, contrived solely to amuse, or to answer some particular purpose; and too many have been the dupes of implicit faith, without examining the affair with that jealous attention which it required. It is not improbable, that in many instances, hobgoblin stories may be explained by the deceptive powers of ventriloquism. We have had auricular demonstration of the extraordinary powers of ventriloquists; they can counterfeit the voices of animals and all imaginable noises, at pleasure, and conjure up a ghost or witch on any occasion. Although ventriloquism was not practised, as an art, in ancient times, it was not unknown, and individuals possessing that faculty might have put it in operation, on particular occasions, without suspicion. In most cases of supposed apparitions and spectres, the reports originated with timorous and credulous persons, or those of questionable character. The scene is always exhibited in the night, when the eye is prepared to see frightful spectres, and the imagination is awaked to magnify every object, whether real or unreal.

> *'All things are full of horror and affright,*
> *And dreadful even the silence of the night.'*

The darkness of the night, the gloom and horror produced by the report of haunted houses, or some disastrous occurrence, as murder or robbery in a particular situation, and a state of mind naturally depressed and melancholy, have doubtless contributed to give a currency to many of those legendary stories which have been credulously received and disseminated by the vulgar. Those, especially, who are trembling with a guilty conscience, are liable to deception; even the most intrepid have been alarmed, when in the night, posts, trees, and other objects, have been presented in a distorted form. We are familiar with the story of the frightened person, who, on passing a church-yard in the night, conceited that he saw a ghost clothed in white; but on examination it proved to be no other than a white horse. A few years ago, Dr Stearns was travelling from Boston to Salem in the evening, having a considerable sum of money about him. He suffered himself to be strongly impressed with the apprehension of being robbed. While his mind was wrought up to the highest pitch, he imagined that a robber approached him with a club suspended over his head, and demanded his money. He instantly took out his pocket book and threw it on the ground, and in great affright drove off with all speed. Having procured assistance and lights, they visited the spot in search of the robber, when to their surprise they found a pump standing near the road, having its handle turned upwards, and the doctor's pocket book instead of being in the hands of a robber, was found lying beside the pump.

Were all the supposed apparitions and spectres to be met with the intrepidity displayed in the following instance, ghost stories would seldom be repeated. About the latter part of the last century, a Mr Blake, of Hingham, Massachusetts, was passing the church-yard in the night, when he saw an object in human form, clothed in white, sitting near an open tomb. Resolving to satisfy himself, he walked toward it. The form moved as he approached, and endeavored to elude his pursuit; when he ran, the object ran before him, and after turning in different directions, descended into the tomb. Mr Blake followed, and there found a woman, who was in a deranged state of mind, who had covered herself with a sheet, and was roaming among the silent tombs.

The passion of fear is implanted in our nature for wise purposes. It prompts us to self defence and the avoidance of evil. It is excited into action by various causes, depending on the condition of the nerves in different constitutions, or in the same at different times. But when extended to imaginary objects of terror, fear becomes superstition, as by a sort of instinct, and has a direct tendency to cherish ignorance and credulity. Dr Franklin had no faith in apparitions and spectres, but he proposed to a friend, that the one which should die first, should return in spirit and visit the survivor; his friend died first, but his spirit never returned. The strong mind of Dr Samuel Johnson was not altogether free from agitation and embarrassment, when contemplating the question of the appearance of incorporeal spirits in our world. This great man said to Mr Boswell, his biographer, 'it is wonderful that 5000 years have now elapsed since the creation of the world, and still it is undecided whether or not there has ever been an instance, in modern times, of the spirit of any person appearing after death. All argument is against it, but all belief is for it.' Boswell suggested, as an objection, that if spirits are in a state of happiness, it would be a punishment to them to return to this world; and if they are in a state of misery, it would be giving them a respite. Johnson replied, that 'as the happiness or misery of spirits depends not upon place, but is intellectual, we cannot say, that they are less happy or less miserable, by appearing upon earth.' Johnson observed, that he makes a distinction between what a man may experience by the mere strength of his imagination, and what imagination cannot possibly produce. Thus, said he, 'suppose I should think that I saw a form, and heard a voice say, Johnson, you are a very wicked fellow, and unless you repent, you will certainly be punished; my own unworthiness is so deeply impressed upon my mind, that I might imagine I thus saw and heard, and therefore I should not believe that an external communication had been made to me. But, if a form should appear, and a voice should tell me, that a particular man had died at a particular place, and a particular hour, a fact which I had no apprehension of, nor any means of knowing, and this fact, with all its circumstances, should afterwards be unquestionably proved, I should in that case be persuaded, that I had supernatural intelligence imparted to me.' Johnson related a story of a ghost, said to have appeared to a young woman several times, advising her to apply to an attorney for the recovery of an old house, which was done, and at the same time saying the attorney would do nothing, which proved to be the fact.

About the middle of the last century, there were reports of a ghost visiting a house in Cocklane, in the city of London. The whole city was, for many weeks, kept in a state of agitation and alarm, and the magazines and newspapers teemed with strange accounts of the Cocklane ghost. The story, at length, became so popular, and created such excitement, as to require a thorough investigation. The purport of the story was, that a spirit had frequently appeared, and announced to a girl, that a murder had been committed near that place, by a certain person, which ought to be detected. For a long time, unaccountable noises, such as knocking, scratching on the walls of the house, &c, were heard every night. The supposed spirit had publicly promised, by an affirmative knock, that it would attend any person into the vault under the church where the body was deposited, and would give a knock on the coffin; it was, therefore, determined to make this trial of the visitation and veracity of the supposed spirit. On this occasion, Dr Johnson, with several clergymen and other gentlemen and ladies, assembled about ten o'clock at night, in the house in which the girl had, with proper caution, been put to bed by several ladies. More than an hour passed, without hearing any noise, when at length the gentlemen were summoned into the girl's chamber, by some ladies who were near her bed, and had heard knocks and scratches. When the gentlemen entered, the girl declared that she felt the spirit like a mouse upon her back. She was required to hold her hands out of bed, and from that time, though the spirit was very solemnly required to manifest its existence by appearance, by impression on the hand or body of any one present, by knocks, or scratches, or any other agency, no evidence of any preternatural power was exhibited. The spirit was then very seriously advertised, that the person to whom the promise was made of striking on the coffin, was then about to visit the vault, and that the performance of the promise was then claimed. The company at 1 o'clock went into the church, and the gentleman to whom the promise was made, went with another into the vault. The spirit was solemnly required to perform its promise, but nothing more than silence ensued. The person supposed to be accused by the spirit then went down with several others, but no effect whatever was perceived. Upon their return they examined the girl, but could draw no confession from her, and the father of the girl, when interrogated, denied in the strongest terms, any knowledge or belief of fraud. It was therefore published by the whole assembly, that the girl had some art of making or counterfeiting a particular noise, and that there was no agency of any higher cause. Thus ended this singular affair, which had so long been permitted to disturb the peace of the city and of the public. The greatest surprise is, that an artful, mischievous girl, should be suffered to set at defiance the closest scrutiny to detect her imposition and deception.

The following anecdote may be found in some historical publication, but is now related from memory without recollecting the authority. After the execution of Charles the First, the Parliament resolved that every vestige of royalty should be annihilated. For this purpose, commissioners were appointed to carry into effect the decree in the Palace of the late King. While executing their prescribed duties, the commissioners were from day to day annoyed and disturbed by strange and frightful noises, in various parts of the house. Logs of wood rolling over the floor in the kitchen, various utensils clattering together, dancing and stamping were heard in rooms whose doors were closed, and to such alarming heights was the deception carried that the commissioners were about to abandon the house, from the belief that it was haunted by evil spirits. At length, on close investigation, the fact was disclosed that the whole deception was the contrivance of a man of singular art, called funny Joe, who was the acting secretary of the commissioners.

In Southey's life of Wesley, we have another instance of supposed preternatural noises in the parsonage house of Wesley's father, in the year 1716. The mysterious noises were said to be as various as unaccountable; such as knocking at the door, lifting up the latch, and a groaning, like a person in distress; a clatter among a number of bottles, as if all at once they had been dashed in pieces; footsteps as of a man going up and down stairs, at all hours of the night; sounds like that of dancing in a room, the door of which was locked; but most frequently, a knocking about the beds at

An Essay on Demonology, Ghosts and Apparitions, and Popular Superstitions

night, and in different parts of the house. Mr Wesley was once awakened a little after midnight, by nine loud and distinct knocks which seemed to be in the next room, with a pause at every third stroke. He and his wife rose, and went below; a noise was now heard, like that of a bag of money poured on the floor at their feet. At one time, the servant heard his hand-mill in rapid motion, without any visible hand to move it. Mr Wesley made every exertion to ascertain the real cause of the noises, without success. He at length became so impatient with the unusual annoyances, that he prepared a pistol, which he was about to discharge at the place where the noise was heard, but was dissuaded from it by a neighboring clergyman, who had been called in to his assistance. But he upbraided the goblin for disturbing the family, and challenged it to appear to him while alone in his study, after which, on entering his study, the door was pressed against him, but no object was seen. At length, the family became so familiar with this invisible spirit, that one of the daughters gave it the name of Old Jeffrey, and they treated it as matter of curiosity and amusement. This unaccountable affair excited much speculation throughout the country. The celebrated Dr Priestley, and many others, undertook to investigate the circumstances, but were unable to make any satisfactory discovery, and it remains inexplicable.

    A reviewer of Wesley's life observes, that few will regard the circumstances as anything more than creatures of imagination, the offspring of credulity and superstition; but I should strongly suspect that some one of the family was the prime mover in the business, as was funny Joe in the Royal Palace of King Charles the First.

James Thacher, M. D., A. A. S.

SUPERSTITION

Historical records furnish innumerable instances of superstition, fraught with circumstances of inexpressible horror. It is an infirmity inherent in our nature, and extremely difficult to eradicate; no lesson on moral evil, or lecture on physical destiny, can sever the spell or dissolve the dark enchantment. So peculiarly fascinating is the love of the marvellous, that when ignorance and bigotry cooperate, the pure fountain of truth is polluted, and the most preposterous tales of antiquity are held in veneration by every fiery zealot. From this cause, millions of innocent lives have been sacrificed. The intellects of thousands have been shackled, and their energies perverted by irrational fears, and by degrading conceptions of the nature of Deity, and of the purposes and modes of religious worship and obedience. It was in the darkest days of superstition, that the rack was in exercise to chain down the understanding, to sink it into the most abject and sordid condition, punishing imaginary crimes, and repressing truth and philosophical research.

The science of medicine had to encounter the scourge of superstition at an early period; the epithet of magician was applied to the physician, who appeared to be endowed with superior genius and knowledge. The inquisition was constantly prepared to take holy cognizance of those who distinguished themselves by extraordinary cures, and hundreds of miserable wretches were dragged to the stake for this cause alone. Galileo, in the 17th century, was condemned by the inquisition to a rigorous punishment, for his noble and useful discoveries in astronomy and geometry; and about the same period, Dr Bartolo suffered a similar fate at Rome, because he unexpectedly cured a nobleman of the gout.

The University of Salamanca decreed that no physician should dare to bleed his patient in a pleurisy in the arm of the affected side; declaring that such practice was of no less pernicious consequences to medicine, than Luther's heresy had been to religion. The inquisition having adopted the irrational and foolish doctrine that diseases should be ascribed to fascination, a physician who opposed that doctrine was compelled to accede to it, and to declare that he had seen a beautiful woman break a steel mirror to pieces, and blast trees by a single glance of her fascinating eyes. Superstitious opinions prevailed in regard to the cure of diseases, also. Some were supposed to be cured by a song. Josephus asserted that he saw a certain Jew, named Eleazer, draw the devil out of an old woman's nostrils, by the application of Solomon's seal to her nose, in the presence of the Emperor Vespasian. Numerous remedies were employed for expelling the devil, among which was flagellation, purgatives, and antispasmodics. Several bewitched persons being cured by a plaster of assafœtida, the question arose, in what way this article excited so much efficacy. Some supposed, that the devil considered so vile an application an insult, and ran off in a passion; but others very sagely observed, that as devils are supposed to have eyes and ears, it is possible that they have noses also, and that it proved offensive to their olfactory nerves. It may be observed that superstition is not confined to those who are ignorant of the laws of the physical world; but through the infirmity of human nature, it has prevailed to the perversion of the profoundest understanding, and the purest intellect. It has arrested the progress of literature and science, and shackled the mind with vulgar fictions, errors, and prejudices. Even the sublime genius of Lord Bacon was subjected to its influence; he believed in witchcraft, and asserted that he was cured of warts by rubbing them with a piece of lard with the skin on, and then exposing it to the sun. Dr More, and the enlightened Cudworth, applied the epithet Atheist to those who opposed the belief of witchcraft. The celebrated Dr Hoffman, the father of the modern theory and practice of medicine, in the large edition of his work in 1742, says, that the devil can raise storms, produce insects, and act upon the animal spirits and imagination; and, in fine, that he is an excellent optician, and natural philosopher, on account of his long experience.

But, blessed be the Almighty Ruler, the present is an era, preeminently distinguished for improvement in physical and moral philosophy; and forgetting the things that are behind, we are pressing forward in the race with rapid strides to the melioration of the condition of the physical and moral world. Had the stupendous works performed, and those contemplated at the present day, been predicted to our fathers in the 17th century, they would have trembled with alarm, lest their posterity were destined to form a league with the infernal powers. The paralyzing idea that the present state of knowledge is as perfect as our nature will admit, should be utterly reprobated; for knowledge is eternally progressive, and we can have no claim to be estimated as the benefactors of posterity, unless by our own efforts and toils we add to the achievements of our ancestors. We may take a retrospect of the meritorious characters of our fathers with exultation, and when disposed to animadvert on the frailties and follies peculiar to their times, let us reflect that it is our happy lot to live in an age in many respects the most glorious the world ever knew. We have a moral interest in all that concerns the human race, and, as philanthropists, we ought to sympathize in every calamity with which our species may be afflicted. Being apprised with what facility mankind deceive themselves, and with what tenacity the mind clings to its darling delusion, sober reflection is awakened to a lively sense of the evils resulting from our imperfections. As the germs of plants may lie dormant in the earth for ages, and be resuscitated, so may the troubles created by unhallowed superstition, revive and be reiterated by means of some depraved spirits in our day.

Ventriloquism is an art which may be made subservient to knavery and deception. An ingenious work on this subject was published in 1772, by M. de la Chapelle, who was of opinion that the responses of many of the oracles were delivered by persons thus qualified to serve the purposes of priestcraft and delusion. That ventriloquism may be made thus subservient to the purposes of knavery, will clearly appear by the following anecdotes.

Louis Brabant, valet de chambre to Francis the First, was a capital ventriloquist, and a great cheat. He had fallen in love with a young, handsome, and rich heiress; but was rejected by the parents as an unsuitable match for their daughter. The young lady's father dying, Brabant made a visit to the widow, who was totally ignorant of his singular talent. Suddenly, on his first appearance, in open day, and in presence of several persons who were with her, she heard herself accosted, in a voice perfectly resembling that of her dead husband, and which seemed to proceed from above, exclaiming, 'Give my daughter in marriage to Louis Brabant. He is a man of great fortune, and of an excellent character. I now endure the inexpressible torments of purgatory for having refused her to him. If you obey this admonition, I shall soon be delivered from this place of torment. You will at the same time provide a worthy husband for your daughter, and procure everlasting repose to the soul of your poor husband.' The widow could not for a moment resist this dread summons, which had not the most distant appearance of proceeding from Louis Brabant, whose countenance exhibited no visible change, and whose lips were closed and motionless, during the delivery of it. Accordingly, she consented immediately to receive him for her son-in-law. Louis's finances, however, were in a very low situation, and the formalities attending the marriage contract, rendered it necessary for him to exhibit some show of riches, and not to give the ghost the lie direct. He accordingly went to work upon a fresh subject, one Cornu, an old and rich banker at Lyons, who had accumulated immense wealth by usury and extortion, and was known to be haunted by remorse of conscience on account of the manner in which he had acquired it. Having contracted an intimate acquaintance with this man, he one day, while they were sitting together in the usurer's little back parlor, artfully turned the conversation on religious subjects, on demons and spectres, the pains of purgatory and the torments of hell. During an interval of silence between them, a voice was heard, which to the astonished banker seemed to be that of his deceased father, complaining, as in the former case, of his dreadful situation in purgatory, and calling upon him to deliver him instantly from thence, by putting into the hands of Louis Brabant, a large sum for the redemption of Christians then in slavery with the Turks; threatening him at the same time with eternal damnation if he did not take this method to expiate likewise his own sins. The reader will naturally suppose that Brabant affected a due degree of astonishment on the occasion, and further promoted the deception, by acknowledging his having devoted himself to the prosecution of the charitable design imputed to him by the ghost. An old usurer is naturally suspicious. Accordingly, the wary banker made a second appointment with the ghost delegate for the next day; and to render any design of imposing upon him utterly abortive, took him into the open fields, where not a house, or a tree, or even a bush was in sight, capable of screening any supposed confederate. This extraordinary caution excited the ventriloquist to exert all the powers of his art. Wherever the banker conducted him, at every step, his ears were saluted on all sides with the complaints and groans not only of his father, but of all his deceased relations, imploring him, for the love of God, and in the name of every saint in the calendar, to have mercy on his soul and theirs's, by effectually seconding with his purse the intentions of his worthy companion. Cornu could no longer resist the voice of heaven, and accordingly carried his guest home with him, and paid him down 10,000 crowns, with which the honest ventriloquist returned to Paris and married his mistress. The catastrophe was fatal. The secret was afterwards blown, and reached the usurer's ears, who was so much affected by the loss of his money, and the mortifying railleries of his neighbors, that he took to his bed and died.

Another French ventriloquist, named M. St Gile, was not less adroit in his secret art. Entering a convent, and finding the whole community in mourning, he inquired the cause, and was told that one of their body had lately died, who was the delight and ornament of the whole society, and they spoke feelingly of the scanty honors they had bestowed on his memory. Suddenly a voice was heard, apparently proceeding from that part of the church where the singing of the choir is performed, lamenting the situation of the defunct in purgatory, and reproaching the brotherhood with their lukewarmness, and want of zeal on his account. The friars, as soon as their astonishment gave them power to speak, consulted together, and agreed to acquaint the rest of the community with this singular event, so interesting to the whole society. M. St Gile, who wished to carry on the joke still farther, dissuaded them from taking this step, telling them that they would be treated by their absent brethren, as a set of fools and visionaries. He recommended to them, however, the immediately calling of the whole community into the church, where the ghost of their departed brother might probably reiterate his complaints. Accordingly, all the friars, novices, lay brothers, and even the domestics of the convent, were immediately summoned and collected together. In a short time the voice from the roof renewed its lamentation and reproaches, and the whole convent fell on their faces, and vowed a solemn reparation. As a first step, they chanted a De profundis in a full choir; during the intervals of which the ghost occasionally expressed the comfort he received from their pious exercises, and ejaculations on his behalf. When all was over, the friar entered into a serious conversation with M. St Gile; and, on the strength of what had just passed, sagaciously inveighed against the absurd incredulity of our modern sceptics and pretended philosophers, on the article of ghosts or apparitions. M. St Gile thought it now high time to disabuse the good fathers. This purpose, however, he found it extremely difficult to effect, till he had prevailed upon them to return with him into the church, and there be witnesses of the manner in which he had conducted this ludicrous deception.

WITCHCRAFT AND SORCERY

A belief in the entity of witchcraft and sorcery may boast of a high degree of antiquity. In both the Old and New Testament, we observe numerous tragical events, bearing the semblance of diabolical agency. A prominent instance is found in the witch of Endor, who is said to have been deeply versed in the art of deception, and notorious in her day for skill in practical astrology. It is the opinion of some divines, that to beguile Saul, she raised a demon, counterfeiting Samuel; but it seems difficult to decide in what precise manner she effected her purpose of imposing upon her credulous employer. The sorcery and witchcraft, prohibited under the Jewish dispensation, is supposed by high authority to be a very different species of crime from that which was so abhorrent in the days of our ancestors; the former might have come under the description of idolatry, or of the heathen mythology. 'The ancients believed that there were good and evil demons, which had influence over the minds of men, and that these beings carried on an intercourse between men and gods, conveying the addresses of men to the gods, and divine benefits to men. Hence, demons became the objects of worship. It was supposed, also, that human spirits, after their departure from the body, became demons, and that the souls of virtuous men, if highly purified, were exalted from demons into gods.'

The various instances of demoniacs, lunatics, and possessed, recorded in the sacred scriptures of the New Testament, have received different interpretations according to the particular views among learned expositors. By some of the enlightened German theologians, those subjects are considered as mere prototypes of the maniacs and epileptics of our own times; but most of the English divines have imbibed different opinions. 'Demoniacs,' says Kenrick, 'were persons disordered in their understandings, and supposed to be possessed by an evil demon.' That real miracles were wrought by our Saviour and his apostles, and that both good and evil spirits were subservient to his will, no Christian believer can ever deny. But by all impartial inquirers after truth, it will perhaps be conceded, that demoniacal possession is a subject the least susceptible of a satisfactory solution, of any in scripture. It has received the most critical investigation of commentators and divines, for centuries, and still remains involved in mystery. The subject in its nature, is too intricate and mysterious to justify even a discussion on this occasion, nor is it requisite for my purpose. It must, therefore, be referred to philosophical commentators and learned biblical critics.

In a work entitled, Historical Essay concerning Witchcraft, by F. Hutchinson, D. D., published in London in 1720, the author says, 'The divine writings, as well as the soundest philosophy and soberest reason, give confirmation that there are both good and bad spirits. There are superior beings intermediate betwixt the divine nature and ours. But both philosophers and Christians that have ventured to define their natures or works, have been very various in their notions respecting them, and the holy scriptures, though they give us many instances of the employment of both the evil and the good spirits, teach us none such as we commonly meet with in the modern relations of witchcraft, and the conjoint powers of Satan. The holy scriptures tell us of no such tales as these which confound the laws of nature, and absolutely destroy the testimony of our senses.' *** 'The human mind is sometimes so clouded and oppressed, that persons think themselves dead. At another time they are elevated far above their natural pitch, full of raptures, and high conceits, and think themselves kings and queens; now if witch stories are in their heads, or witchcraft in their imaginations, why may they not think themselves bewitched, or fancy themselves witches or wizards, as well as kings and queens?'

A witch, in her personal character, was commonly an uncouth old woman, or hag. Her countenance was repulsive, her air and gait disgusting, and her general aspect and movements at variance with a proper demeanor. She is supposed to have formed a compact with the devil, giving herself up to him body and soul. This compact, it is believed, cannot be transacted mentally, but the devil must appear in bodily shape to the witch. In this interview, he delivers to her an imp, or familiar spirit, by which she is enabled to transport herself in the air, on a broomstick or a spit, to distant places in the night to attend witch meetings, at which the devil always presides. She was supposed to be attended by an old gray cat, as her confederate, or imp; the cat and her mistress, it was believed, were often overheard plotting their fairy tricks together. She was supposed to possess the power of transforming herself into a cat, a squirrel, or other animal, which she would send abroad to execute her commands. These animals could not be killed but by a silver bullet, and should the animal receive a wound the witch would have a wound in the same place. It was imagined that the witch, by the aid of Satan, had power to inflict death, and various diseases and evils, on families and individuals, and also on cattle, by way of revenge for any offence, and could even raise storms and tempests, and sink ships at sea.

Numerous legendary tales were formerly propagated of haunted houses, where witches assembled and held their nightly orgies and diabolical revels. These haunts were always objects of great terror to the credulous vulgar, being considered as a pandemonium of all manner of evils, miseries, and calamities. The idea was prevalent, also, that witches could bridle men in the night, and ride them about at pleasure. The woman who should exhibit the characteristics above described, was at once stigmatized as being in league with the devil, and was treated not only with ridicule and contempt, but subjected to unmerciful persecution. Ranked among demons, instruments of the devil, they were objects of no pity, but were viewed with scorn and horror. Instances were not wanting of these wretched mortals, although entirely innocent, becoming so hateful and terrible to all, and befriended by none, that at length they abhorred themselves, and were reconciled to be burnt or hung, that they might escape the rage of cruel persecution.

The methods put in practice for the discovery of witches were various and singular. One was, to weigh the suspected woman against the church bible, which, if she was guilty, would preponderate. Another was to require her to repeat the Lord's prayer; in attempting this, a witch will always hesitate and blunder. If a witch should weep, she could not shed more than three tears, and that out of the left eye. This deficiency of tears was considered as a very substantial proof of guilt. Excrescences on the body, from which the imps receive their nourishment, were deemed infallible signs of a witch. She was bound crosswise, the right thumb tied to the left toe, and the left thumb to the right toe; in this condition she was cast into the water, if guilty she could not sink, for having in her compact with the devil renounced the water of baptism, the water in return refuses to receive her. If she was found able to swim in that condition, she was taken out and burnt or hung; but it is probable the bystanders were allowed to save them from drowning or few could escape. The trial by the stool was resorted to as another expedient; the suspected woman was placed in the middle of the room on a stool cross-legged; if she refused, she was bound with cords, and in this uneasy posture she was kept without meat or sleep, for twentyfour hours, during which it was supposed that her imps would return to her for nourishment. A small hole was left in the door for the imps to enter, and persons were directed to be constantly sweeping the floor, and to keep a strict watch for spiders, flies, or other insects, and if they could not kill them, they certainly were the witch's imps. Suspected witches were sometimes put to cruel torture to force confession, and were afterwards executed. From such kinds of proof, together with the most absurd and foolish evidence of old women and children, thousands of innocent persons were condemned for witchcraft, and burnt at the stake.

Bishop Jewel, in a sermon preached before Queen Elizabeth, in 1558, tells her, 'It may please your Grace to understand that witches and sorcerers, within these last four years, are marvellously increased within your Grace's realm. Your subjects pine away even unto death; their color fadeth, their speech is benumbed, their senses are bereft; I pray God they never practise farther than upon the subject.' John Bell, minister of the gospel at Glaidsmuir, says, 'Providentially two tests appeared to discover the crime. If the witch cries out, "Lord have mercy upon me!" when apprehended, and the inability of shedding tears; because, as a witch could only shed three tears, and those with her left eye, her stock was quickly exhausted; and that was the more striking, as King James I. shrewdly observes, "since other women in general are like the crocodile, ready to weep upon every slight occasion."'

King James the First, indulged a ferocious antipathy against sorcery and witchcraft, and in the first year of his reign, a new statute was passed, embracing every possible mode and form in which imagination could paint the mystical crime. James fully considered his own personal safety greatly endangered, as attempts had been made to poison him by some who practised the magic art. He composed a book on demonology, in which he advised the water ordeal, by swimming, and when a work was published in opposition to his opinion and desire, he ordered it to be burnt by the common executioner.

That illustrious English lawyer, Sir William Blackstone, having, in his commentaries on the laws of England, stated the evidence on both sides of the question, concerning the reality of witchcraft, says, 'It seems to be the most eligible way to conclude that, in general, there has been such a thing as witchcraft, though one cannot give credit to any particular modern instance of it.' According to our conceptions of human actions, they are in general prompted and governed by reason, and perhaps most frequently the dominant motives are those which pertain to our own individual interest. Now it may be inquired in what imaginable circumstances the interest of human beings can be linked with the affairs of Satan, or their welfare promoted by his influence? No one will pretend, that there can be honor attached to a seat in his privy council, for it is well known that a witch is considered one of the most odious and despicable wretches in existence. Nor will it be contended that pecuniary advantages are derivable from that source; wizards and witches are always poor, miserable, forlorn beings. They are supposed to give themselves up to serve under the banners of a cruel, tyrannical master, the implacable enemy and tempter of mankind, whose very name excites horror and detestation in every virtuous mind. It must, however, be confessed that a strong bias to scepticism relative to things we cannot understand, is no less a mark of weakness of intellect, than indiscriminate credulity. But I am aware, that the real existence of the fraternity has received the credence of some of the wisest and best of men. Divine providence has permitted the delusion respecting this great scourge to prevail in the minds of some, as he did the sin of idolatry among his chosen people while in their pilgrimage to the land of promise.

Numerous instances of imposition and counterfeit have been detected in times of alarm from supposed witchcraft. There are in all countries those who cannot exist but in times of confusion and civil commotion. They delight to be noticed as objects of great wonder and curiosity, and when they cannot be distinguished for virtuous actions, resort to deeds of the most infernal character, according to their own interest, passion, or capricious humor. They learn to counterfeit various kinds of fits; bark and snarl like a dog, goggle their eyes, foam at the mouth, distort their bodies, and disjoint their limbs. Such impostors have their confederates or partners who join with them, and share in the profit, or in the humor.

Dr Francis Hutchinson, published a chronological detail of trials and executions for supposed witchcraft, sorcerers, and conjurors, in various countries in Europe. From this it will be seen, he observes, that, in all ages of the world, superstitious credulity has produced greater cruelties than are practised among Hottentots, or other nations whose belief in a Deity is called in question. The number of witches and their supposed dealings with Satan, he observes, will increase or decrease according as such doings are accounted probable, or impossible. Under the former supposition, charges and convictions will be found augmented in a terrific degree. When the accusations are disbelieved and dismissed as not worthy of attention, the crime becomes unfrequent, ceases to occupy the public mind, and affords little trouble to the judges. That where the times have not been so violent and superstitious but that sensible men might venture to speak freely, and the accused could have a fair trial, they have usually discovered cheat and imposture. Fifteen famous detections of fraud were made, many of them after judges and juries, and a multitude of eye witnesses had been deceived. Had the rest undergone as strict inquiry, most of them would probably have proved innocent.

In the year 1427, the famous heroine Joan of Arc, after her glorious military exploit at the siege of Orleans, being taken prisoner by the Earl of Bedford, was cruelly burnt as a witch. In 1488, a violent tempest of thunder and lightning in Spain, having destroyed the corn for some leagues around, the people accused two old women of being the cause. They confessed and were burnt. Other instances, no less preposterous, are recorded about that period. In 1515, five hundred persons were executed at Geneva, in three months, as witches and wizards, and at another place, fortyeight were burnt in five years. Eighteen were condemned in England in 1596; an account of their trials was published, with the names and colors of the spirits. A perusal of that fantastic production must have excited wonder and amazement in any age.

In France, in 1594, the crime of witchcraft had become so common, that the jails were not sufficient to contain the prisoners, nor had they judges enough to try them. In 1595, a woman was hanged in England, for sending an evil spirit into Thomas Darling; and E. Hartley was executed for bewitching seven persons. In the trial, spectral evidence was made use of against him, and the experiment of saying the Lord's prayer, which it was believed a witch is unable to repeat. But that which touched his life, was a deposition that he had made the magic circle for conjuration. In 1612, twelve women were executed at Lancaster. Mary Smith believed herself to be a witch, and died very pious. A learned and eminent clergyman in France, named Grandier, was, in 1634, put to cruel torment on suspicion of an evil spirit, and was adjured to clear himself by shedding tears if innocent. He was tortured till he swooned on the rack, and then inhumanly burnt. From 1634 to 1661, history records accounts of several hundreds executed in England, of both sexes, husband and wife, mother and daughter together, some confessing, others declaring themselves innocent. In Germany, whole counties were depopulated, that no witch might escape. But it was in Scotland that Satan was set at liberty to execute his vengeance. There the floodgates of malice, revenge, and bloodshed, were thrown open, and multitudes were swept away by the dreadful torrent. No less, it is said in history, than 4000 victims were cruelly sacrificed within a short period, for the dubious crime which never has and never can be proved. In 1664, two women were tried before the celebrated Lord Chief Justice Sir Matthew Hale, and were convicted. The evidence against the accused was so trivial, that his Lordship was greatly embarrassed on the occasion, and his scruples

James Thacher, M. D., A. A. S.

were such, that he declined the duty of summing up the evidence. Being willing, however, that the law should have its course, he pronounced sentence, and they were executed. The evidence against them was, partly spells and partly spectral, and one evidence was that a cart run against the cottage of one of the women, by which she was offended, and shortly after the same cart stuck fast in a gate where its wheels touched neither of the posts, and yet was moved easily forward on one of the posts being cut down. A girl, supposed to be bewitched, went into a fit on being touched by one of the accused. But much weight was given to the evidence of Sir Thomas Browne, 'that the fits were natural, but heightened by the power of the devil, cooperating with the malice of witches.' (Sir Walter Scott, page 225.) About this period, seventy persons were condemned in Sweden, and most of them executed. Fifteen children were also executed, thirtysix ran the gauntlet, and twenty were whipped for the same reputed crime. In 1678, six were executed in Scotland for bewitching Sir George Maxwell. The principal evidence in these cases was a deaf and dumb girl, who made signs that there was a picture of wax in one of their houses as an instrument of enchantment, but it was proved afterwards that it was placed there by herself, and she was whipped through the streets of the city and banished. In 1682, three women were hung at Exeter, confessing themselves witches, but died with pious prayers in their mouths. These were the last executed in England for the crime of witchcraft. Some of the accused persons were in their indictments charged with keeping imps, one was said to be like a pole-cat. On one trial several witnesses deposed that the grandmother and aunt of the prisoner were hanged for witches, and that her grandmother had said that she had eight or nine imps, and that she had given two or three to each of her children. In 1697, about twentyeight were accused in Scotland, by a girl eleven years old. Two boys and a girl, and two other persons, saved themselves by confessing, and upon their testimony seven were executed, all denying their guilt.

A notorious witch-finder, says Dr Increase Mather, undertook by a pin to make an infallible discovery of suspected persons. If, when the pin was pushed an inch or two into the flesh, no blood appeared, nor any sense of pain, then he declared them to be witches. No less than three hundred persons, says that respectable author, were thus condemned in that kingdom. This miscreant was Matthew Hopkins, who styled himself witch-finder general, and travelled from town to town with a train of assistants, for the professed purpose of detecting witches, charging twenty shillings for each town. He affected to have uncommon skill in his profession, but treated his subjects with great cruelty, keeping them from sleep, wearying them to distress by constant walking to force confession. He also adopted the mode of swimming them while cross-bound. But the cruel wretch finally met his just deserts; he was treated as he had treated hundreds of others, being thrown into the water cross-bound; but, although able to swim as a witch, he was suffered to escape from the country. It is greatly to be lamented, that a considerable number of Calvinistic divines should take zealous concern in the prosecution of reputed witches. Among those pious divines, we find the venerable names of Baxter and Calamy, in England, and the two Mathers in America. That they were conscientious, and influenced by the purest motives, no one will doubt; but that they were imbued with a large share of the credulity of the times, will appear most evident. The following are Mr Baxter's own words as quoted by Sir Walter Scott. 'The hanging of a great number of witches in 1645 and 1646, is famously known. Mr Calamy went along with the judges on the circuit, to hear their confessions, and see there was no fraud or wrong done them. I spoke with many understanding, pious, learned, and credible persons, that lived in the counties, and some that went to them in the prisons, and heard their sad confessions. Among the rest an old reading parson, named Lewis, was one that was hanged, who confessed that he had two imps, and that one of them was always putting him upon doing mischief; and he being near the sea, as he saw a ship under sail, it moved him to send it to sink the ship; and he consented, and saw the ship sink before them.' The Rev. Mr Lewis was condemned on his own simple confession, that he sent his imp to sink a ship, but it was not known that any ship was lost, and it was supposed that the man was deranged in his intellect. Mr Baxter relates another story of a mother, who gave her child an imp like a mole, and told her to keep it in a can near the fire, and she would never be in want.

The Catholic priests were remarkable for their zealous pretensions to peculiar powers in dispossessing demons, by fasting and prayer, and they were detected in numerous frauds. It was probably from their reports that the story originated which Dr Mather cites in his cases of conscience, that at the time when Martin Luther died, all the possessed people in the Netherlands became quiet and at ease. The devils in them said the reason was, that Luther had been a great friend of theirs, and they owed him so much respect as to go as far as Germany to attend his funeral, and on the mention of some ministers of the reformed religion, the devils in the possessed laughed and said, that they and the Calvinists were very good friends. There were among the Protestants some clergymen base enough to become rivals with papists in their pretended exorcisms. The following is an instance of unprecedented turpitude. In 1689, Richard Dugdale, of Lancaster, was reported by a clergyman as having been dispossessed of devils, by fasting and prayer. He had for several months exhibited, at intervals, apparent sufferings, both surprising and unaccountable. He would counterfeit the demoniac, epileptic, and a train of nervous fits, and unnatural afflictions, which were attributed to demons. His singular condition excited the curiosity and wonder which he and his vile minister desired, and his supposed sufferings called forth the sympathy, and his indigent circumstances the charity of his numerous deluded visitors. By these means he was encouraged to persevere in his deception, living at ease on the delusion which he and his minister had artfully created about a year. When at length complaint was made to the Bishop of London, who brought Dugdale to confess that he had acted the part of an impostor, and that he had, from time to time, received private lessons of instruction from the clergyman, to carry on the imposition, that he might have the credit of dispossessing the devil, by his fastings and prayers.

In the trials for witchcraft, says Dr Hutchinson, an unpardonable partiality was manifested, owing to the vulgar prejudices among the people. The English statute against witchcraft and sorcery interdicts all acts of sorcery whatever, and all charms for employing spirits; yet, for discovering a reputed witch, the accusers were allowed to use charms which must have their force, if any at all, from the same diabolical power. This is unprecedented partiality, and directly contrary to the statute. Whether such compacts are real or imaginary, they ought to be punished equally on both sides. The number of witches, and the supposed dealings of spirits, have been found to increase and decrease according to the laws and principles subsisting at the time and place. Since philosophy and learning have prevailed, we have had but little trouble about witches and sorcerers, except that created by the superstitious imagination of men. We may have as many devils in our day as they had in other ages, for we have as many murders, robberies, false accusations, and lies, and other crimes which are the devil's works. Some are of opinion that the devil cannot really control the laws of nature, while others aver, that the laws of nature are a mere jest with him. It has been denied that he possesses power to transform a man or woman into a cat, but Dr Henry More believed he could, and describes the manner in which he transforms them. It is difficult to conceive how Dr More acquired such knowledge; but we shall never believe that Satan is the ruler of our world. We have no reason to imagine that God has endowed him with miraculous powers; he cannot, therefore, impart such powers to others; consequently, there can be no such creature as a witch. All illusive fancies of witchcraft may be clearly explained on the principles of mental philosophy and sound and enlightened reason. The confessions of witches have so often been extorted, so often the effects of distraction, and so often been found contrary to plain truth and sober reason, that no dependence should be placed on them. Dr Hutchinson asserts, that it may be plainly proved, from scripture and reason, that there never was a witch, such as we mean, who can send devils, diseases, and destruction, among the people. The spectral evidence made use of in courts, is far from being legal proof, it is of no sort of weight, nor should it be regarded as anything more than dreams. The confessions of ignorant old women, ought to have been entirely rejected; some were extorted, many were impossible, and all ridiculous and incredible.

The Rev. Dr Holmes, in his American Annals, observes, that our fathers, before the world was enlightened by learning and philosophy, loved to astonish themselves with the apprehensions of witches and prodigies, charms and enchantment. There was not a village in England, he observes, that had not a ghost in it; the church-yards were all haunted, every large common had a circle of fairies belonging to it, and there was scarce a shepherd to be met with who had not seen a spirit.

The dreadful contagion was at length permitted to afflict the puritans of New England, and our revered ancestors were involved in a series of tragical events, and overwhelmed with the most appalling apprehensions. A retrospect to that sorrowful period creates painful impressions; but however revolting the transactions in those days of melancholy delusion, we are not without the consoling hope, that our pious fathers were guided by a conscientious spirit in their proceedings and condemnations. The people of New England were naturally of a grave and serious cast, and remarkably prone to the most rigid and sacred construction on all the events of Providence, and too often their sentiments were biassed by enthusiasm and superstition. The books containing narratives of trials of witches and sorcerers in England, had been received here, and could not fail of making a deep impression on the public mind. Hence it is not strange that there should be a close coincidence between the English witches and those reputed such in New England, and that they should suffer a similar fate. So violent was the popular prejudice against every appearance of witchcraft, that it was deemed meritorious to denounce all that gave the least reason for suspicion. Every child and gossip were prepared to recognise a witch, and no one could be certain of personal safety. As the infatuation increased, many of the most reputable females, and several males also, were apprehended and committed to prison. There is good reason to believe, that, in some instances, the vicious and abandoned, availed themselves of opportunities of gratifying their corrupt passions of envy, malice, and revenge. The English judge, Sir Matthew Hale, so eminently distinguished for his knowledge in the law, and his exemplary piety, was most highly estimated here, and knowing that he had condemned some persons in England, his opinion had great influence with both judges and

James Thacher, M. D., A. A. S.

juries.

    In a publication in 1767, by the Rev. John Hale, of Beverly, it appears that the first person who suffered in New England for witchcraft was a woman in Charlestown; and in the collection of the Massachusetts Historical Society, (Vol. V. second series) it is recorded, that 'in June 1648, one Margaret Jones of Charlestown, was executed for a witch. She was proved to have such a malignant touch, that whomsoever she touched with any affection of displeasure, were taken presently after with deafness, vomiting, or other violent sickness. Soon after she was executed, a ship riding over against Charlestown, of three hundred tons, having in her hold an hundred and twenty tons of ballast, and eighty horses aboard her for the Barbadoes, was on a sudden observed to roll as if she would have turned over. The husband of that witch lately executed had desired passage in that ship to Barbadoes, which not obtaining, that accident was observed to follow. Notice being given of this to the magistrates, then sitting in court at Boston, a warrant was sent to apprehend him, and as the officer was passing therewith over the ferry, one asked if he could not tame the vessel, seeing he could sometimes tame men; he answered, I have that here, which, it may be, will tame her and make her quiet, showing his warrant, and at the same instant, the ship began to stop her motion, and swim upright, which had continued rolling, after a strange manner about twelve hours, and after Jones was in prison she never moved in that kind any more.'

    Another, executed not long after, was a Dorchester woman; she also positively denied being guilty. The next was a woman of Cambridge, against whom a principal evidence was a nurse, who testified that the accused did bewitch a child to death; for the woman made much of the child, being perfectly well, but quickly changed its color, and it died in a few hours after. The woman denied her guilt to the last moment. In 1655, Mrs Hibbens, widow of an assistant, or counsellor, was executed at Boston. This gave great dissatisfaction to several principal persons, and it was believed that her death saved the lives of many other inferior persons. About the same time, two or three at Springfield, and one at Hartford, were executed, two of whom confessed themselves guilty. The next that suffered was in 1662, a woman named Greensmith, and her husband with her; who confessed, but he denied guilt. Two other were put to the water ordeal, but being found to float on the water like cork, were permitted to fly from New England. This ridiculous experiment appears to have been soon after abandoned. In 1663, Mary Johnson was tried and hanged. She said the devil appeared to her, and cleaned her hearth of ashes, and hunted the hogs out of the corn. In 1688, a female named Glover, an Irish papist, was hung for bewitching four children of one John Goodwin, of Boston. This affair was attended by such extraordinary circumstances as to arrest a general interest and sympathy. Goodwin was a man of unexceptionable moral character, and his children were religiously educated, and discovered mild and amiable tempers. 'These children,' says the celebrated Dr Cotton Mather, 'were arrested by a stupendous witchcraft. The eldest, a daughter thirteen years old, was first seized with odd fits, in appearance diabolical; it was not long before one of her sisters, and two brothers, were similarly affected.' They were at times deaf, dumb, and blind. Their tongues would be drawn down their throats, and then pulled out upon their chins. Their mouths were thrown open with great violence, and then the jaws clapped together again with a force like that of a spring lock, and all their limbs and joints were strangely distorted. They made piteous outcries that they were cut with knives, and struck with blows. The ministers of Boston and Charlestown, had recourse to fasting and prayer, and during the devotions, the children it is said were deprived of hearing; but the youngest child was entirely relieved. The poor ignorant woman, above mentioned, was suspected of employing demons to afflict these children; she was arrested, and committed to jail in chains. On her trial she rather bragged than denied her guilt, but she would converse only in Irish, though she understood the English language very well. Her house being searched, several images and puppets, or babies made of rags and stuffed with goat's hair, were found, and she confessed that her way to torment the objects of her malice, was by wetting her finger with spittle and stroking those little images. The afflicted children were present in court, and the woman appeared to be greatly agitated. One of the images being presented to her, she oddly and quickly snatched it into her hand, and instantly one of the children fell into a fit. The judges ordered a repetition of the experiment, with the same result. Being asked if she had any one to stand by her as a friend, she replied that she had, and looking round in the air, she added, no, he is gone. The night after, she was heard expostulating with the devil for his deserting her, telling him that because he had served her so basely and falsely, she had confessed all. The court appointed several physicians to examine whether she was in any degree crazed in her intellect; but they pronounced her sane, and the court passed sentence of death upon her, and she was executed. After the condemnation of the woman, Dr Mather made her many visits; she declined answering his questions, or attending to his prayers, pretending that her spirits would not consent to it. At her execution she said the afflicted children should not be relieved by her death, as others were concerned in it; accordingly the three children continued to be tormented. They frequently discerned spectres around them, and when a blow was aimed at the place where they saw the spectre, the boy always felt the blow in the part of his body answering to that stricken at, and it was very credibly affirmed that a dangerous woman or two in the town, received blows thus given to their spectres. At length, the children would bark at each other like dogs, and pur like so many cats. They would complain that they were in a hot oven, or roasting on an invisible spit, and that knives were cutting them. They would complain of blows from a great cudgel, and though we could see no cudgels, we could see the marks of the blows in red streaks upon their skin. They would complain that their heads were nailed to the floor, and it required more than ordinary strength to pull them from thence. They would be so limber sometimes, that it was judged every bone might be bent, and anon so stiff, that a joint could not be moved. Sometimes they would fly like geese, with incredible swiftness, through the air, their arms waving, like the wings of birds, and the feet scarcely touching the ground once in twenty feet. The sight of the Bible, and all religious discourse, would throw them into distressing fits. Dr Mather took the eldest of these children into his own family, that he might have opportunity to observe the doings of Satan more critically; but unhappily his own imagination was so continually haunted by ideas of wicked demons and witches, that he was unconscious of the imposition he was suffering. When he prayed, her hands with a strong force would be clapped upon her ears, and if pulled away by force she would cry out. She complained that she had Glover's chain round her leg, and would imitate her in her gait. An invisible chain would be clapped about her, and she would, in much pain and fear, cry out when they put it on. Sometimes we could with our hands knock it off as it began to be fastened. But when it was on she would be pulled out of her seat, with such violence that it was difficult to keep her out of the fire. I may add, says the learned, but credulous doctor, that the demons put an unseen rope with a cruel noose about her neck, by which she was choked till she was black in the face, and though it was got off before it killed her, yet there were the red marks of it, and of a finger and thumb, remaining for some time. She once said, if she could steal or get drunk, she would be well. At one time an invisible horse was brought to her, and she would put herself in the posture of a riding woman. She would in her chair throw herself into a riding posture, sometimes ambling, sometimes trotting, and sometimes galloping very furiously, and attempting to ride up stairs. Dr Mather observes, that the girl having learned that he was about to prepare a sermon on the occasion of the witchcraft, became very turbulent and insolent, constantly endeavoring to interrupt his studying the sermon. In prayer time, the demons would throw her on the floor, where she would whistle and sing to drown the voice, and attempt to kick and strike the speaker. But to conclude this tedious story. At Christmas, says the doctor, this girl and her sister in another house, were by the demons made very drunk, though the people in the house were well satisfied that it was without strong drink. They imitated, with wonderful exactness, the actions of one drunk in speaking, and reeling, and vomiting, and anon sleeping, till they recovered. These children were all restored to their natural health, and lived to adult age. Governor Hutchinson, in his History of Massachusetts, says he was acquainted with the eldest daughter; she sustained an unblemished character; but he believes she never made any confession of fraud or imposition in this transaction.

Hutchinson was truly an excellent historical writer, whatever may have been his political principles and conduct as chief magistrate. From the history and from the collections of the Historical Society, I copy the following narrative, with the view of evincing to what extent artful children may impose on credulous persons.

In the year 1720, there was at Littleton, in the county of Middlesex, a family who were supposed to be bewitched. One J. B. had three daughters, eleven, nine, and five years old. The eldest was a forward and capable girl, and having read and heard many strange stories, would surprise the company by her manner of relating them. Pleased with the applause, she went from some she had heard to some of her own framing, and so on to dreams and visions, and attained the art of swooning, and of being, to all appearance, breathless. Upon her revival she would relate strange things she had met with in this and other worlds. When she met with the word God, and other solemn words in the Bible, she would drop down as if dead. Strange and unaccountable noises were often heard in, and upon the house, stones came down the chimney and did considerable mischief. She complained of the spectre of Mrs D--y, a woman in the town, and once she desired her mother to strike at a place where she said there was a yellow bird, and she said to her mother, you have hit the side of its head, and it appeared that Mrs D--y's head was hurt about the same time. Another time the mother struck at the place where the spectre was, and the girl said, you have struck her on the bowels, and on inquiry it was found, that Mrs D--y complained of a hurt on her bowels about the same time. It was common to find her in ponds of water, crying out she should be drowned; sometimes upon the top of the house, and again upon the tops of trees, pretending she had flown there, and some fancied they had seen her in the air. There were often the marks of blows and pinches upon her, which were supposed to come from an invisible hand. The second daughter, after her sister had practised the art for some months, and had succeeded so well, imitated her in complaints of Mrs D--y, and outdid her in feats of climbing the barn and trees, ascending where she could not descend without assistance with a ladder. What was most surprising, the youngest, of five years old only, attempted the same feats and in some instances went beyond her sisters. The neighbors agreed they were under an evil hand, and it was pronounced witchcraft, as certain as there ever had been at Salem. Physicians had been at first employed, but to no purpose, and afterwards ministers and elders were called to pray over them, but without success. The children had numerous visitors, and the more they were pitied, the more loud and constant were their moans and distractions; few spectators suspected that they were acting the part of perverse and wicked impostors. The afflicted parents treated them with all possible care and tenderness, believing that they were objects of pity and compassion. At length Mrs D--y, not long after the supposed blows from the mother, sickened and died, and the two oldest girls ceased complaining; the youngest held out longer, but all persisted in it that there had been no fraud. But their consciences, that inward monitor, finally severely lashed and tortured them. The eldest, for some years, wore a gloominess upon her mind, and when questioned by her parents and others on the subject, she would artfully turn the discourse. Not having been baptised, she applied to a minister for baptism, who examined her closely relative to the affair, telling her she was suspected of falsehood and fraud; but this she denied and asserted her innocence. In 1728, having removed to Medford, she applied to Rev. Mr Turell, to be admitted into his church. She gave him a very good account of the state of her soul, and discoursed sensibly and religiously respecting her past temper and conversation in life. Mr Turell knew nothing of her having been an actor in the fraud above detailed, and propounded her for full communion. The next Sabbath, without any reference to her, he happened to preach from this text, 'He that telleth lies shall not escape.' The day before she was to be admitted into the church she visited Mr Turell in great distress and anguish of mind, inquiring of him what dreadful things he had heard about her, that made him preach so awfully against the practice of lying and liars. Mr Turell being much surprised, replied that no one had made any complaint against her and that he had no particular reference to her. With great grief she frankly confessed that she had been a great sinner, but was now awakened and convinced by the word preached, and that she was resolved no longer to conceal the truth, but confess it before God and man. She then proceeded to acknowledge herself guilty of the wicked deception which she had practised, bewailing and weeping bitterly for her egregious folly and wicked conduct. She then desired Mr Turell to draw up a suitable confession to be read before the congregation, and she would publicly own and acknowledge the same; which was accordingly done, and she was admitted to full communion, and ever after conducted in a manner becoming the Christian profession. She acknowledged to Mr Turell as follows: that the motives which excited her and her sisters to act the part of impostors, were from folly and pride. Finding that she pleased others or caused admiration, she was over pleased with, and admired herself, grew conceited and high minded. She thought to be able to deceive her parents and neighbors, was a fine accomplishment. She never dreamed of witchcraft in her case. The wounds, pinches, and bruises on their bodies, were from their own hands, and the noises and stones falling down the chimney, were the effects of their contrivance. She was often sorry she ever began the deception, but could not humble herself to desist, and was obliged to tell one lie to hide another. Her two sisters, she said, seeing her pitied had become actors also, with her, without being moved to it by her; but when she saw them follow her, they all joined in the secret and acted in concert, and thus during eight months their parents were kept in constant painful anxiety, and they were considered as objects of pity and compassion. They had no particular spite against Mrs D--y, but it was necessary to accuse some person, and the eldest having pitched upon her, the others followed. The woman's complaints about the same time the girl pretended she was struck, proceeded from other causes which were not then properly inquired into. Once, at least, they were in great danger of being detected in their tricks; but the grounds of suspicion were overlooked through the indulgence and credulity of their parents.

SALEM WITCHCRAFT

    I shall now detail an impartial history of the memorable trials and executions for supposed witchcraft at Salem, in 1692. A controversy respecting the settlement of a minister had subsisted in Salem for some time prior to this melancholy catastrophe. They had also recently been deprived by death of several of their most distinguished and influential characters, who had been considered as the fathers and governors of the town for half a century. Unfortunately, two or three ministers in the town, and several in the vicinity, were, with a large proportion of the inhabitants, bigoted and superstitious believers in the doctrine of witchcraft, and they aggravated the general prejudice and fanaticism. From preconceived opinions and strong prejudices, it was scarcely possible that the trials should be impartially conducted. It seemed not to be recollected, that in the trials of witches no other evidence should be received than in the trials of murderers and other criminals; and that no convictions should be made, but through the most substantial human testimony, rejecting all diabolical or witch evidence, which can, on no principle, be deemed legal in any case. In the language of the late Dr Bentley, in his History of Salem, 'The spark fell upon inflammable matter, and behold, how great a matter a little fire kindleth.' But it would be unjust not to make due allowance for the times in which they lived, and the melancholy delusions which prevailed from the war of prejudice, and the slavish effects of the most imbecile apprehensions. These errors, like those of a thousand years ago, are equally opposed to the progress of knowledge, and to a pious confidence in the wisdom and goodness of an Almighty Providence. The authorities from which the following history is derived, are, Hutchinson's History of Massachusetts, Dr Cotton Mather's Magnalia, Wonders of the Invisible World, by the same author, Historical Collections, and More Wonders of the Invisible World, by R. Calef, of Boston, published in 1700.

    In a letter of Thomas Brattle, F. R. S., dated October 8, 1692, published in the Collections of the Massachusetts Historical Society, we have the following account.

    'As to the method which the Salem justices do take in their examinations, it is truly this; a warrant being issued out to apprehend the persons that are charged and complained of by the afflicted children as they are called, said persons are brought before the justices, the afflicted being present. The justices ask the apprehended why they afflict those poor children, to which the apprehended answer, they do not afflict them. The justices order the apprehended to look upon the said children, which, accordingly, they do; and at the time of that look (I dare not say by that look, as the Salem gentlemen do) the afflicted are cast into a fit. The apprehended are then blinded and ordered to touch the afflicted; and at that touch, though not by that touch (as above) the afflicted do ordinarily come out of their fits. The afflicted persons then declare and affirm, that the apprehended have afflicted them; upon which the apprehended persons, though of never so good repute, are forthwith committed to prison on suspicion for witchcraft.'--'Such was the excess of their stupidity, that to the most dubious crime in the world, they joined the most uncertain proofs.'--'A person ought to have been a magician to be able to clear himself from the imputation of magic.'

    The first instance of reputed witchcraft in the town of Salem, took place in the family of Mr Parris, minister of Salem, and very soon after, one or two in the neighborhood were afflicted in a similar manner, and a day of prayer was kept on the occasion. The persons who complained of being afflicted, were a daughter and a niece of Mr Parris, girls of ten or eleven years of age; and these were soon followed by two other girls. They made similar complaints, and exhibited antic gestures and tricks, similar to those of Goodwin's children, two or three years before. The physician, unable to account for the complaint, pronounced them bewitched. They named several women whose spectres they saw in their fits, tormenting them, and in particular Tituba, an Indian woman belonging to Mr Parris's family. She had been trying some experiments, which she pretended to be used in her own country, in order to find out the witch; upon this, the children cried out against the poor Indian as appearing to them, pinching, pricking, and tormenting them, and they fell into fits. Tituba acknowledged that she had learned how to find out a witch, but denied that she was one herself. Several private fasts were kept at the minister's house, and several more public by the whole village, and then a general fast through the colony. This probably had a tendency to bring the afflicted into notice; which, with the pity and compassion of those who visited them, encouraged and confirmed them in their designs, and increased their numbers. Tituba, as she said,

James Thacher, M. D., A. A. S.

being beat and threatened by her master to make her confess, and to accuse her sister witches, as he termed them, did confess that the devil urged her to sign a book, which he presented, and also to work mischief with the children, and she was sent to jail. The children complained, likewise, of Sarah Good, who had long been counted a melancholy or distracted woman, and also Sarah Osborn, an old bedridden woman, both of whom being examined by two Salem magistrates, were committed to jail for trial. About three weeks after, two other women of good character, and church members, Corey and Nurse, were complained of and brought to their examination, when these children fell into fits, and the mother of one of them joined with the children and complained of Nurse as tormenting her, and made most terrible shrieks, to the amazement of all the neighborhood. The old women denied everything charged against them, but were sent to prison; and such was the infatuation, that a child of Sarah Good, about four or five years old, was committed also, charged with being a witch and of biting some of the afflicted, who showed the print of small teeth on their arms; and all that the child looked upon, it is said, fell down in fits, complaining that they were in torment. Elizabeth Proctor, being accused and brought to examination, her husband, as every kind husband would have done, accompanied her to her examination; but it cost the poor man his life. Some of the afflicted cried out against him, also, and they both were committed to prison. Instead, says Governor Hutchinson, of suspecting and sifting the witnesses, and suffering them to be cross-examined, the authorities, to say no more, were imprudent in making use of leading questions, and thereby putting words into their mouths, or suffering others to do it. Mr Parris was over-officious; most of the examinations, although in the presence of one or more of the magistrates, were taken by him. They allowed of such as the following trivial replies to their examining questions. John the Indian. 'She hurt me, she choked me, and brought the book a great many times. She took hold of my throat, to stop my breath. She pinched and bit me till the blood came. I saw the witches eat and drink at such a place, and they said it was their sacrament; they said it was our blood, and they had it twice that day.' Upon such kind of evidence, persons of blameless character were committed to prison; and, such was the dreadful infatuation, that the life of no person was secure. The most effectual way to prevent an accusation was to become the accuser; and accordingly the number of the afflicted increased every day, and the number of the accused in proportion; who, in general perished in their innocence. More than a hundred women, many of them of fair characters and of the most reputable families, in the towns of Salem, Beverly, Andover, Billerica, &c, were apprehended, examined, and generally committed to prison. Goodwife[A] Corey, as she was called, was examined before the magistrates, in the meeting-house in the village; the novelty of the case produced a throng of spectators. Mr Noyes, one of the ministers of Salem, began by prayer. Several children and women were present, that pretended to be bewitched by her, and the most of them accused her of biting, pinching, and strangling, and said that they did, in their fits, see her likeness coming to them, and bringing a book for them to sign. She was accused by them, that the black man, meaning the devil, whispered to her now while she was on her examination. The unfortunate woman could only deny all that was laid to her charge, and she was committed to jail. A miserable negro slave was accused by some of the girls, but on examination she extricated herself by her native cunning. Question to Candy. 'Are you a witch?' Answer. 'Candy no witch in her country. Candy's mother no witch. Candy no witch, Barbadoes. This country, mistress give Candy witch.' 'Did your mistress make you a witch in this country?' 'Yes, in this country mistress give Candy witch.' 'What did your mistress do to make you a witch?' 'Mistress bring book, and pen, and ink, make Candy write in it.' From this testimony, Mrs Haskins, the mistress, had no other way to save her life but to make confession.

In April, 1692, there was a public hearing and examination before six magistrates and several ministers. The afflicted complained against many with hideous clamors and screechings. On their examinations, besides the experiment of the afflicted falling down at the sight of the accused, they were required to repeat the Lord's Prayer, which it was supposed a real witch could not do. When Sir William Phipps entered upon the office of Governor, in May, 1692, he ordered the witches to be put in chains; upon that it was said the afflicted persons were free from their torments. In May, Mrs Carey, of Charlestown, was examined and committed. Her husband published the following facts.

'Having for some days heard that my wife was accused of witchcraft, and being much disturbed at it, we went to Salem by advice to see if the afflicted knew her. The prisoners were called in before the justices, singly, and as they entered were cried out against by the afflicted girls. The prisoners were placed about seven or eight feet from the justices, and the accusers between the justices and the prisoners. The prisoners were ordered to stand directly before the justices with an officer appointed to hold each hand lest they should therewith afflict the girls; and the prisoners' eyes must be constantly fixed on the justices; for if they looked on the afflicted, they would either fall into these fits, or cry out of being hurt by them; after examination of the prisoners, who it was that afflicted these girls, &c, they put them upon saying the Lord's Prayer as a trial of their guilt. When the afflicted seemed to be out of their fits, they would look stedfastly on some one person, and not speak, and then the justices said they were struck dumb, and after a little time they would speak again; then the justices said to the accusers, which of you will go and touch the prisoner at the bar? Then the most courageous would venture, but before they made three steps would fall on the floor as if in a fit. The justices then ordered that they should be taken up and carried to the prisoner, that she might touch them, and as soon as this was done the justices would say they are all well, before I could discern any alteration, but the justices seemed to understand the manner of the strange juggle. Two of the accusers who pretended to be bewitched, were Abigail Williams, niece of Mr Parris, aged eleven or twelve years, and Indian John, the husband of Tituba, who was now in jail. This fellow had himself been accused of witchcraft, but had now become an accuser for his own safety. He showed several old scars which he said were the effects of witchcraft, but more likely of the lash. On inquiry who they would accuse as the cause of their sufferings, they cried out Carey, and immediately a warrant was sent by the justices to bring my wife before them. Her chief accusers were two girls; my wife declared to the justices that she never had any knowledge of them before that day. She was obliged to stand with her arms extended. I requested that I might hold one of her hands, but it was denied me. She then desired that I would wipe the tears and the sweat from her face and that she might lean herself on me as she was faint; but justice Hathorn said she had strength enough to torment those persons, and she should have strength enough to stand. I remonstrated against such cruel treatment, but was commanded to be silent, or I should be turned out of the room. Indian John was now called in to be one of the accusers; he fell down and tumbled about like a brute, but said nothing. The justices asked the girls who afflicted the Indian; they answered she, (meaning my wife); the justices ordered her to touch him in order to his cure; but her head must be turned another way, lest instead of curing, she should make him worse by looking on him; her hand was guided to take hold of his, but the Indian seized hold of her hand, and pulled her down on the floor, in a violent manner; then his hand was taken off, and her hand put on his, and the cure was quickly wrought. My wife, after being thus cruelly treated, was put into prison, and the jailor was ordered to put irons on her legs which weighed about eight pounds. These chains, with her other afflictions, soon produced convulsion fits, so that I was apprehensive she would have died that night. I intreated that the irons might be removed, but in vain. I now attended the trials at Salem, and finding that spectre evidence, together with idle or malicious stories, was received against the lives of innocent people, I trembled for the fate of my wife; as the same evidence that would serve for one would serve for all. In this awful situation, I thought myself justifiable in devising some means of escape; and this, through the goodness of God, was effected. We were pursued as far as Rhode Island, but we reached New York in safety, where we were kindly received by Governor Fletcher. To speak of the treatment of the prisoners and the inhumanity shown them at their executions, is more than any sober Christian can endure. Those that suffered, being many of them church members, and most of them of blameless conversation.--Jonathan Carey.'

 Captain John Alden, of Boston, mariner, was sent for by the magistrates of Salem, upon the accusation of several poor, distracted, or possessed creatures, or witches. On his examination, these wretches began their juggling tricks, falling down, crying out, and staring in the faces of people; the magistrates demanded of them several times who it was of all the people in the room, that hurt them; one of the accusers pointed several times to one Captain Hill, but said nothing, till a man standing behind her to hold her up, stooped down to her ear, when she immediately cried out, Alden, Alden afflicted her. Being asked if she had ever seen Alden, she answered no, but she said the man told her so. Alden was then committed to custody, and his sword taken from him, for they said he afflicted them with his sword. He was next sent for to the meeting-house, by the magistrates, and was ordered to stand on a chair to the open view of all the assembly. The accusers cried out that Alden pinched them when he stood on the chair; and one of the magistrates bid the marshal hold open his hands, that he might not pinch those creatures. Mr Gidney, one of the justices, bid Captain Alden confess, and give glory to God. He replied, he hoped he should always give glory to God, but never would gratify the devil. He asked them why they should think that he should come to that village to afflict persons that he had never seen before; and appealed to all present and challenged any one to produce a charge against his character. Mr Gidney said he had known him many years, and had been to sea with him, and always believed him to be an honest man; but now he saw cause to alter his opinion. Alden asked Gidney what reason could be given why his looking upon him did not strike him down as well as the miserable accusers; but no reason could be given. He assured Gidney that a lying spirit was in his accusers, and that there was not a word of truth in all they said of him. Alden, however, was committed to jail where he continued fifteen weeks, when he made his escape. At the examinations, and at other times, it was usual for the accusers to tell of the black man, or of a spectre, as being then on the table; the people present would strike with swords or sticks at those places. One justice broke his cane at this exercise; and sometimes the accusers would say they struck the spectre; and it was even reported that several of the accused women were hurt and wounded thereby, though at home at the same time.

James Thacher, M. D., A. A. S.

In June and July, the court of Oyer and Terminer proceeded on trials and condemnations, and six miserable creatures were executed, protesting their innocence.

At the trial of Sarah Good, one of the afflicted girls fell into a fit, and after coming out of it, she cried out against the prisoner for stabbing her in the breast while in court, and actually produced a piece of the blade of the knife which she said was used and broken in doing it. Upon this, a young man was called to prove the imposition. He produced a haft and part of the blade, which the court, having viewed and compared, found to be the same; and the young man affirmed, that yesterday he happened to break that knife, and that he cast away the upper part in the presence of the person who now produced it. The girl was cautioned by the court not to tell any more lies, but was still employed to give evidence against the prisoners whose lives were in her hands.

Mr Noyes, the minister, urged Sarah Good to confess, saying he knew she was a witch, and she knew she was a witch; to which she replied, 'You are a liar. I am no more a witch than you are a wizard.' At the trial of Rebecca Nurse it was remarkable that the jury brought her in not guilty; immediately all the accusers in the court, and soon after all the afflicted out of court, made a hideous outcry, to the amazement of the court and spectators. The court having expressed some dissatisfaction, the jury were induced to go out again to consider better one expression of hers when before the court. They now brought her in guilty, and she was condemned. After her condemnation, she was by Mr Noyes of Salem, excommunicated and given to the devil. The governor, however, saw cause to grant a reprieve, upon which, when known, the accusers renewed their dismal outcries against her, insomuch that the governor was by some Salem gentlemen prevailed with to recall the reprieve, and she was executed with the rest. The testimonials of her Christian behaviour, both in the course of her life, and at her death, are numerous and highly satisfactory. Mary Easty, her sister, was also condemned. She was of a serious and religious character, and before her execution she presented a petition to the court and the reverend ministers at Salem, protesting her innocence before God. She petitioned, not for her own life, for she knew she must die; but most earnestly prayed, that if possible, no more innocent blood might be shed. By her own innocence she said she knew the court was in the wrong way, and humbly begged that their honors would examine the confessing witches, being confident that many of them had belied themselves and others. They had accused her and others, she said, of having made a league with the devil, which she and they most positively denied. 'The Lord alone, who is the searcher of all hearts, knows that as I shall answer it at the tribunal seat, that I know nothing of witchcraft, therefore I cannot, I dare not, belie my own soul by confessing.' She intreats their honors not to deny the humble petition of a poor, dying, innocent person, and prays that the Lord will give a blessing to their endeavors that no more innocent blood be shed. These two women were among the eight who were executed together, when the Rev. Mr Noyes, turning towards the bodies, said, what a sad thing it is to see eight firebrands of hell hanging there!!

John Proctor, while confined in prison, complained that two young men were compelled to a confession by being tied neck and heels till the blood was ready to burst out of their noses. They then confessed that one had been a wizard a month, and the other five weeks, and that their mother had made them so when she had been confined in jail without seeing them for nine weeks. He adds, 'My son, William Proctor, when he was examined, because he would not confess that he was guilty, they tied him up neck and heels till the blood gushed out of his nose.'

At a court held in Salem, April, 1692, by the honorable Thomas Danforth, deputy governor, Elizabeth Proctor was tried for witchcraft. The witnesses were Indian John, husband to Tituba, and three or four girls who pretended to be afflicted by the said Proctor. The questions by the court, and the answers of the witnesses, were exceedingly futile and whimsical; but they exhibited their antic gestures and fits, which they pretended were caused by the presence of the prisoner at the bar. The court then put the question thus--'Elizabeth Proctor, you understand whereof you are charged, viz. to be guilty of sundry acts of witchcraft: what say you to it?' 'Speak the truth as you will answer it before God another day. What do you say, Goody Proctor, to these things?' 'I take God in heaven to be my witness, that I know nothing of it, no more than a child.' Proctor, the husband, being present in court, the afflicted girls cried out against him, saying he was a wizard, and again exhibited their tricks and fits. The question was put by the court, 'Who hurts you?' Answer. 'Goodman Proctor, and his wife too.' By the court. 'What do you say, Goodman Proctor, to these things?' 'I know not, I am entirely innocent.' It is no less painful than astonishing to add that by such miserable evidence, Proctor and his wife were both condemned and executed. Proctor earnestly entreated that he might be allowed a few days to prepare himself for death, and at his execution he desired in the most affecting manner that Mr Noyes would pray with, and for him; but his request was cruelly denied him, because he would not confess himself to be a wizard.

August 19th, 1692, five persons were executed, all protesting their innocence in the firmest manner. One of this number was Mr George Burroughs, who had been a preacher several years before at Salem village, where there had been some misunderstanding between him and the people;

afterwards he became a preacher at Wells. It was alleged against Mr Burroughs, that he had been seen to perform feats of strength exceeding the natural powers of man. He had lifted a barrel of molasses or cider from a canoe, and carried it to the shore. He would, with one hand, extend a heavy musket of six or seven feet barrel, at arm's length. In addition to these charges, it was urged by the writers of that day, as a principal part of the evidence, that seven or eight of the confessing witches witnessed against him. But it will appear from the examinations by the court, that their evidence was drawn from them. For example. Question to Mary Lacey. 'Was there not a man among you at your meetings?' 'None but the devil.' 'Your mother and grandmother say there was a minister there; did you not see men there?' 'There was a minister there, and I think he is now in prison.' 'Was there not one Mr Burroughs there?' 'Yes.'--Question to another witness. 'Were there not two ministers there?' 'I heard Sarah Good talk of a minister or two, one of them is he that has been to the eastward; his name is Burroughs.' Margaret Jacobs had been brought to accuse herself of being a witch, and then to charge Burroughs the minister, and her own grandfather, but afterwards being struck with horror, she chose to lose her own life rather than persist in her confession. She begged forgiveness of Burroughs before his execution, who is said to have freely forgiven her; and to have prayed with, and for her. She also recanted all she had said against her grandfather, but all in vain as to his life. Some of the accusers asserted that Burroughs often attended the witch or devil's sacrament. Some testified, that, in their torments, Burroughs tempted them to go to a sacrament; and he would, with the sound of a trumpet, summon other witches; who, quickly after the sound, would come from all quarters unto the rendezvous. Numerous other charges, equally frivolous, were brought against this unfortunate minister, as stated by Dr Cotton Mather; among others, his venomous bites, leaving the prints of his teeth upon the flesh, which would compare precisely with his set of teeth. It is seldom that a man, 80 years of age, can boast a good set of teeth, and some said that he had not one in his head, and could be no other than imaginary teeth, but these could answer their purpose. Burroughs had been twice married, and it was reported of him, perhaps truly, that he had treated his wives unkindly.

'Several of the bewitched,' adds Dr Cotton Mather, 'gave in their testimony that they had been troubled with the apparitions of two women, who said they were Burroughs' two wives, and that he had been the death of them, and that the magistrates must be told of it, before whom, if Burroughs upon his trial denied it, they did not know but they should appear against him in court. Burroughs being now on trial, one of the bewitched persons was cast into horror at the ghosts of the two deceased wives, then appearing before him, and crying for vengeance against him. But he, though much appalled, utterly denied that he discerned anything no of it: nor was this,' adds Dr Mather, 'any part of his conviction.'[B] It was testified by some of the witnesses, that the prisoner had been at witch meetings with them; and that he was the person who had seduced them into the snares of witchcraft; that he promised them fine clothes for doing it; that he brought puppets to them, and thorns to stick into those puppets, for the afflicting of other people; and that he exhorted them with the rest of the crew to bewitch all Salem village, but be sure to do it gradually, if they would prevail in what they did. It was testified of one Ruck, brother-in-law to the prisoner, that himself and sister, with Burroughs, going out two or three miles to gather strawberries, Ruck, with his sister, rode home very moderately with Burroughs on foot in company. Burroughs stepped aside into the bushes, whereupon they halted and holloed for him. He not answering, they proceeded homewards with a quickened pace, and yet, when they were got near home, to their astonishment they found him on foot with them, having a basket of strawberries. Burroughs then fell to chiding his wife for speaking to her brother of him on the road; which, when they wondered at, he said he knew their thoughts. Ruck being startled at that, intimated that the devil himself, did not know so far. Burroughs answered, 'My God makes known your thoughts unto me.' The prisoner at the bar had nothing to answer unto what was thus witnessed against him, that was worth considering. 'But the court began to think,' says Dr Mather, 'that he then stepped aside only that by the assistance of the black man he might put on his invisibility, and in that fascinating mist, gratify his own jealous humor to hear what they said of him.' This is paying no great compliment to the philosophical character of the court. Burroughs was, however, condemned, and was carried in rags in a cart through the streets of Salem, to his execution; and his body was dragged by the rope over the ground, and buried among some rocks, one hand and part of the face left uncovered. When on the ladder, he repeated the Lord's Prayer; probably because it was the popular opinion, that a wizard is deprived of the power of doing it, and he also protested against the injustice of his sufferings with such awful solemnity, as to affect the spectators to tears, and it was by some apprehended that the populace would have prevented the execution. He suffered this ignominious death at the age of about 80 years, with fervent prayers that the dreadful delusion might cease. As soon as he was turned off, Dr Cotton Mather, being mounted, addressed himself to the people, declaring that Burroughs was not an ordained minister, and that there was the fullest proof of his guilt. Dr Increase Mather, equally credulous in these things with his son, in his "Cases of Conscience," affirms, that he was present at the trial of Burroughs, and had he been one of his judges, he could not have acquitted him. 'For several persons did on oath testify, that they saw him do such things as no man that has not a devil to be his familiar, could perform.'

John Willard was another who suffered about the same time. He had been employed in looking up witches, but at last refusing to fetch in more, as he deemed it unjust, he was accused. He at first made his escape to a distance of forty miles, but was overtaken and condemned. Giles Corey, aged about 80 years, was brought to trial, but refused to plead, being unwilling to be tried by a jury that cleared no one; he was therefore pressed to death. When in the agonies of death, the victim thrust out his tongue, and the officer pushed it into his mouth with his cane. This was the first, and I believe the only one, who was pressed to death in New England, though there had been examples of it in Old England. Corey's wife suffered at the gallows, where she made an eminent prayer.

September 22d, eight were executed, the horse carrying them together in a cart to the gallows, failed for a short time, and the accusers said the devil hindered it; but it may be asked, if he had power to arrest the cart for a moment, why not stop it altogether, and prevent the executions? But they shew no signs of confidence or hope in his power to save them. One Wardwell, having formerly confessed himself guilty and afterwards denied it, was brought upon his trial. His former confession and spectre evidence were adduced against him; but his own wife and daughter accused him and saved themselves. 'There are,' says Hutchinson, 'many instances of children accusing their parents, and some, of parents accusing their children. This is the only instance of a wife or husband accusing one the other, and surely this instance ought not to have been suffered. I shudder while I relate it.' Besides these irregularities, there were others in the course of these trials. At the execution of Wardwell, while he was speaking to the people, protesting his innocence, the executioner being at the same time smoking his pipe, the smoke coming in his face interrupted his discourse, the accusers said the devil hindered him with smoke.

Mrs English was a woman of superior mind, and an excellent education; but was thought not to be very condescending or charitable to the poor; and by some of them she was accused of witchcraft. The officer read to her the warrant in the evening, and guards were placed round her house. In the morning, after attending the devotions of the family, she kissed her children with great composure, proposed her plan of education, and took leave of them, and told the officer she was ready to die, being confident that would be her fate. After being examined, she was by indulgence committed to custody in a public house, where her husband frequently visited her, and this occasioned an accusation against him. Being a man of large property, a merchant in Salem, and having considerable influence, he fortunately obtained permission to be confined with his wife in a prison in Boston, till the time of trial. Here their friends found means to effect their escape, and they fled to New York, where they were received with friendly attention by Governor Fletcher. In the winter following, Mr English sent generous supplies to the suffering poor at Salem; but on his return after the storm had subsided, he found his house plundered, and his property so reduced, that from an estate valued at £1500, he realized only about £300.

In July, one Goody Foster was examined before four justices. She had confessed many things of herself, but her daughter now confessed others in which she was concerned. She was told that her daughter was with her when she rode on the stick, and was with her at the witch meetings, and was asked how long her daughter had been engaged with her. She replied that she had no knowledge of it at all. She was then told that one of the afflicted persons said, that Goody Carryer's shape told her that Goody Foster had made her daughter a witch about thirteen years ago. She replied that she knew no more about her daughter's being a witch, than what day she should die. If I knew anything more I would speak it to the utmost. The daughter being called in, and asked whether she had any discourse with her mother while riding on the stick, replied, I think not a word. Next comes the important question by the magistrate, 'Who rid foremost on that stick to the village?' 'I suppose my mother.' The mother replied, 'no, Goody Carryer was foremost.' It might be supposed that it was time for the magistrates to stop; but they proceed to question the daughter. 'How many years since they were baptized, who baptized them, and how?' 'Three or four years I suppose; the old serpent dipped their heads in the water, saying they were his, and that he had power over them forever and ever.' 'How many were baptized that day, and who were they?' 'I think there were six, some of the chiefs, they were of the higher powers.' The old woman's granddaughter, M. Lacey, was now called in, and instantly M. Warren fell into a violent fit, but was soon restored when Lacey laid her hand on her arm. Question by the justices. 'How dare you come in here and bring the devil with you to afflict these poor creatures; which way do you do it?' 'I cannot tell. If my mother made me a witch I did not know it.' She was now directed to look on M. Warren in a friendly way, without injuring her; but in doing so she struck her down with her eyes. Being asked if she would now acknowledge herself to be a witch, she said yes. Being asked how long, she said she had not been a witch above a week. The devil appeared to her in the shape of a horse, bidding

37

her worship him, and fear nothing, and he would not bring her out, but he has proved a liar from the beginning. The questions being still put to her, she again said, she had been a witch but a little more than a week; but at another time she replied, that the devil appeared to her a little more than a year ago for the first time.

Among other persons accused of witchcraft, was Mrs Hale, whose husband, the minister of Beverly, had been very active in these prosecutions; this was a stroke which the good man was not prepared to receive. Being fully satisfied of his wife's innocence, the question was now suggested and controverted, whether the devil could afflict in a good person's shape, taking it for granted, that the minister's wife was a good person. The accusation of Mrs Hale, and some others of respectable character, brought them to believe that the devil could so manage matters as that the afflicted person should think he did. This affair effected a considerable alteration in the sentiments and conduct of Mr Hale. He became much more moderate and rational in his views of witchcraft. In the midst of their distress and confusion, the clergymen of the town and vicinity held a consultation by request of the governor and council, upon the state of things as they stood; particularly, to consider the question, whether Satan may not appear in the shape of an innocent and pious, as well as of a nocent and wicked person, to afflict such as suffer by diabolical molestation? They reported, among other things, as their opinion, 'That presumptions, whereupon persons may be committed, and much more, convictions, as being guilty of witchcraft, ought certainly to be more considerable than barely the accused person's being represented by a spectre unto the afflicted; inasmuch as it is an undoubted and notorious thing, that a demon may by God's permission appear even to ill purposes, in the shape of an innocent, yea, of a virtuous man. Nor can we esteem alterations made in the sufferers by a look or touch of the accused, to be an infallible evidence of guilt, but frequently liable to be abused by the devil's legerdemain.'

Among the confessing witches were D. Falkner, a child of ten years, A. Falkner, of eight, and S. Carryer, between seven and eight. Sarah Carryer's confession. It was asked by the magistrates. 'How long hast thou been a witch?' 'Ever since I was six years old.' 'How old are you now?' 'Near eight years old; brother Richard says I shall be eight years old next November.' 'Who made you a witch?' 'My mother. She made me set my hand to a book. I touched it with my fingers, and the book was red, the paper was white.' Being questioned she said she never had seen the black man, the place where she did it was in a pasture, and her aunt T. and her cousins were there. They promised to give her a black dog, but the dog never came to her. 'But you said you saw a cat once, what did that say to you?' 'It said it would tear me in pieces if I would not set my hand to the book.' She said her mother baptized her, and the devil or black man was not there as she saw. She said she afflicted people by pinching them, she had no puppets, her mother carried her to afflict. 'How did your mother carry you when she was in prison?' 'She came like a black cat.' 'How did you know it was your mother?' 'The cat told me she was my mother.' This poor child's mother was then under sentence of death, and the mother of the other two children was in prison also, and was soon after tried and condemned.

The following is among the affecting instances of confessors retracting their confessions.

The humble declaration of Margaret Jacobs unto the honored court now sitting at Salem, showeth, 'That whereas your poor and humble declarant, being closely confined in Salem jail, for the crime of witchcraft, which crime, thanks be to the Lord, I am altogether ignorant of, as will appear at the great day of judgment. May it please the honored court, I was cried out upon by some of the possessed persons, as afflicting them; whereupon I was brought to my examination, which persons at the sight of me fell down, which did very much startle and affright me. The Lord above knows I knew nothing in the least degree who afflicted them; they told me without doubt I did, or they would not fall down at seeing me; they told me if I would not confess, I should be put down into the dungeon, and would be hanged; but if I would confess I should have my life spared; the which did so affright me, that to save my life, I did make the confession, which confession, may it please the honored court, is altogether false and untrue. The very first night after, I was in such horror of conscience that I could not sleep, for fear the devil would carry me away for telling such horrid lies. I was, may it please the honored court, sworn to my confession, as I understand since, but at that time I was ignorant of it, not knowing what an oath did mean. The Lord, I hope, in whom I trust, out of the abundance of his mercy, will forgive me my false forswearing myself. What I said was altogether false against my grandfather and Mr Burroughs, which I did to save my life and to have my liberty; but the Lord charging it to my conscience, made me in so much horror, that I could not contain myself before I had denied my confession; choosing rather death with a quiet conscience, than to live in such horror. And now, may it please your honors, I leave it to your pious and judicious discretion, to take pity and compassion on my young and tender years, to act and to do with me as the Lord and your honors shall see good; having no friend but the Lord to plead my cause, not being guilty in the least measure of the crime of witchcraft, nor any other sin that deserves death from the hands of man.'

James Thacher, M. D., A. A. S.

The horrid scourge of witchcraft was, by means of the imprudence, or rather the folly, of an individual, extended to the town of Andover. One Joseph Ballard, of that town, sent to Salem for some of the accusers who pretended to have the spectral sight to tell him who afflicted his wife, who was then sick of a fever. Soon after this, fifty persons at Andover were accused of witchcraft, many of whom were among the most reputable families. Here the nonsensical stories of riding on poles through the air, were circulated. Many parents believed their children to be witches, and many husbands their wives, &c.

The following is the grand jury's bill against Mary Osgood.

'The jurors for our sovereign Lord and Lady the King and Queen present, that Mary Osgood, wife of Captain Joseph Osgood, of Andover, in the county of Essex, about eleven years ago, wickedly, maliciously, and feloniously, a covenant with the devil did make, and signed the devil's book, and took the devil to be her God, and consented to serve and worship him, and was baptized by the devil, and renounced her former christian baptism, and promised to be the devil's, both body and soul, forever, and to serve him; by which diabolical covenant by her made with the devil, she, the said Mary Osgood, is become a detestable witch, against the peace of our sovereign Lord and Lady the King and Queen, their crown and dignity, and the laws in that case made and provided.'

The foregoing bill was grounded principally on her own confession, the purport of which is as follows.--That about eleven years ago, when she was in a melancholy state, upon a certain time while walking in her orchard, she saw the appearance of a cat at the end of her house, which she supposed was a real cat, about this time she made a covenant with the devil, &c. She said further, that about two years agone, she was carried through the air in company with three others, whom she named, to five mile pond, where she was baptized by the devil, and was transported back again through the air in the same manner in which she went, and believes they were carried on a pole. She confesses that she had afflicted three persons, and that she did it by pinching her bed clothes, and giving consent the devil should do it in her shape, and that the devil could not do it without her consent. When in court, she afflicted several persons, as they pretended, and they were as usual restored by her touching their hands. It was not long after, that the said Mary Osgood, with five other women, who had, when in danger, confessed themselves guilty, retraced their confessions, stating that 'they were blind-folded, and their hands were laid on the afflicted persons who fell into fits; others when they felt our hands, said they were well, and that we were guilty of afflicting them, whereupon we were committed to prison. By reason of that sudden surprisal, knowing ourselves perfectly innocent, we were exceedingly astonished and amazed, consternated and afflicted out of our reason. Our nearest and dearest friends and relations, seeing our awful situation, entreated us to make confession, as the only way to save our lives. They, out of tender love and pity, persuaded us to make such confession, telling us we were witches, they knew it, and we knew it, and they knew that we knew it, which made us think it was really so. Our understanding and reasoning faculties almost gone, we were incapable of judging of our condition. Some time after, when we had been better composed, they telling us what we had confessed, we did profess we were innocent, of such things.' The testimonials to these persons' characters, says Governor Hutchinson, by the principal inhabitants of Andover, will outweigh the credulity of the justices who committed, or of the grand jury which found bills against them. Fiftythree reputable inhabitants of Andover, addressed the court, held at Salem, stating that 'they are women of whom we can truly give this character and commendation, that they have not only lived among us so inoffensively as not to give the least occasion to suspect them of witchcraft, but by their sober, godly, and exemplary lives and conversation, have obtained a good report in the place, where they have been well esteemed and approved in the church, of which they are members.'

One Dudley Bradstreet, a justice of peace in Andover, having himself committed thirty or forty persons to prison for supposed witchcraft, himself and wife were both accused, and they were obliged to flee for their lives. The accusers reported, that Mr Bradstreet had killed nine persons, for they saw the ghosts of murdered persons hover over those that had killed them. A dog being afflicted at Salem, those that had the spectral sight said, that J. Bradstreet, brother of the justice, afflicted the dog and then rode upon him. He also was glad to make his escape, and the dog was killed. Another dog was said to afflict others, and they fell into fits when the dog looked on them, and he was killed. At length a worthy gentleman of Boston, being accused by some of those at Andover, sent a writ to arrest the accusers in a thousand pound action, for defamation. From that time the accusations at Andover generally ceased, to the unspeakable joy of the inhabitants.

This tremendous storm continued sixteen months in Salem, in which was displayed a great want of sober wisdom in some, and of moral honesty in others, while a spirit of superstitious persecution, almost without a parallel, generally prevailed. Nineteen innocent persons were hanged, one pressed to death, and eight more condemned; and about fifty confessed themselves witches, of which not one was executed. Above one hundred and fifty were in prison, and above two hundred more, being accused, it was thought proper to put a stop to further prosecutions. The persons in the prisons were set at liberty, and those who had fled returned home in peace. Experience showed that the more were apprehended, the more were afflicted by Satan, and the number of confessors increasing, increased the number of the accused; and the executing of some made way for the apprehension of others, till the numbers became actually alarming to the public, and it was feared that Salem had involved some innocent persons, as all the nineteen denied the crime to their death.

The late Dr Bentley of Salem, in his History of that town, published in the Historical Society's Collections, observes, that 'the scene was like a torrent, sudden, irresistible, and momentary. They who thought they saw the delusion, did not expose it, and they who were deluded were terrified into distraction. For a time no life was safe. On the trials, children below twelve years of age obtained a hearing before magistrates. Indians came and related their own knowledge of invisible beings. Tender females told every fright, but not one man of reputation ventured to offer a single report, or to oppose openly the overwhelming torrent. Nothing could be more ridiculous than a mere narrative of the evidence. It would be an affront to the sober world. The terror was so great, that at the hazard of life, they who were charged with guilt confessed it, and the confessions blinded the judges. The public clamors urged them on, and the novelty of the calamity deprived them of all ability to investigate its true causes, till nineteen innocent persons were made victims to the public credulity.' 'From March to August, 1692,' says Dr Bentley, 'was the most distressing time Salem ever knew; business was interrupted, the town deserted, terror was in every countenance, and distress in every heart. Every place was the subject of some direful tale, fear haunted every street, melancholy dwelt in silence in every place after the sun retired. The population was diminished, business could not, for some time, recover its former channels, and the innocent suffered with the guilty. But as soon as the judges ceased to condemn, the people ceased to accuse. Terror at the violence and the guilt of the proceedings, succeeded instantly to the conviction of blind zeal, and what every man had encouraged, all now professed to abhor. Every expression of sorrow was found in Salem. The church erased all the ignominy they had attached to the dead, by recording a most humble acknowledgment of their error. But a diminished population, the injury done to religion, and the distress of the aggrieved, were seen and felt with the greatest sorrow.'

I quote the following from Judge Story's Centennial Discourse.

'The whole of these proceedings exhibit melancholy proofs of the effects of superstition in darkening the mind, and steeling the heart against the dictates of humanity. Indeed nothing has ever been found more vindictive and cruel than fanaticism, acting under the influence of preternatural terror, and assuming to punish offences created by its own gloomy reveries. Under such circumstances it becomes itself the very demon whose agency it seeks to destroy. It loses sight of all the common principles of reason and evidence. It sees nothing around it but victims for sacrifice. It hears nothing but the voice of its own vengeance. It believes nothing but what is monstrous and incredible. It conjures up every phantom of superstition, and shapes it to the living form of its own passions and frenzies. In short, insanity could hardly devise more refinements in barbarity, or profligacy execute them with more malignant coolness. In the wretched butcheries of these times, (for so they in fact were,) in which law and reason were equally set at defiance, we have shocking instances of unnatural conduct. We find parents accusing their children, children their parents, and wives their husbands, of a crime, which must bring them to the scaffold. We find innocent persons, misled by the hope of pardon, or wrought up to frenzy by the pretended sufferings of others, freely accusing themselves of the same crime. We find gross perjury practised to procure condemnations, sometimes for self protection, and sometimes from utter recklessness of consequences. We find even religion itself made an instrument of vengeance. We find ministers of the gospel and judges of the land, stimulating the work of persecution, until at last in its progress its desolations reached their own firesides.'

There are not wanting, Hutchinson observes, those who are willing to suppose the accusers to have been under bodily disorders, which affected their imaginations. This is kind and charitable, but seems to be winking the truth out of sight. A little attention must force conviction, that the whole was a scene of fraud and imposture, commenced by young girls, who at first, perhaps, thought of nothing more than exciting an interest in their sufferings, and continued by adult persons, who were afraid of being accused themselves. Rather than confess their fraud, they permitted the lives of so many innocent persons to be sacrificed. None of the pretended afflicted were ever brought upon trial for their fraud; some of them proved profligate persons, abandoned to all vice, others passed their days in obscurity and contempt.

In December, 1696, there was a proclamation for a fast, in which there was this clause, 'That God would shew us what we know not, and help us wherein we have done amiss, referring to the late tragedy raised among them by Satan and his instruments, through the awful judgment of God.' On the day of the fast, at the South meeting-house in Boston, Judge Sewall, who had sat on the bench at the trials, delivered in a paper to be read publicly, and he stood up while it was reading. It expressed in a very humble manner, that he was apprehensive he might have fallen into some error in the trials at Salem, and praying that the guilt of such miscarriages may not be imputed either to the country in general, or to him or his family in particular, and asking forgiveness of God and man. The Chief Justice, Mr Stoughton, being informed of this action of one of his brethren, observed for himself, that when he sat in judgment, he had the fear of God before his eyes, and gave his opinion according to the best of his understanding; and although it might appear afterwards that he had been in an error, yet he saw no necessity of a public acknowledgment of it.

Twelve men who had served as jurors in court at Salem, in 1692, published a recantation of their sentiments, and an apology for their doings on the trials; stating that they were incapable of understanding, nor able to withstand the mysterious delusions of the powers of darkness, and the prince of the air, but for want of knowledge and information from others, took up such evidence against the accused as, on further consideration and better information, they justly fear they have been instrumental with others, though ignorantly and unwittingly, to bring upon themselves the guilt of innocent blood, &c. They express a deep sense of sorrow for their errors in acting on such evidence to the condemnation of persons, declaring with deep humility that they were deluded and mistaken, for which they are much distressed and disquieted in mind. They humbly beg forgiveness of God, and praying that they may be considered candidly and aright by the surviving sufferers, acknowledging themselves under the power of strong and general delusion. They again ask forgiveness of all whom they may have offended, declaring they would not do such things again for the whole world.

As this great calamity began in the house of Mr Parris, and he had been a witness and very zealous prosecutor of the supposed offenders, many of his church withdrew from his communion, and in April, 1693, they drew up articles against him. 'They charge the said Parris of teaching such dangerous errors, and preaching such scandalous immoralities as ought to discharge any man, though ever so gifted otherwise, from the work of the ministry. Particularly, in his oath against the lives of several, wherein he swears, that the prisoners with their looks knock down those pretended sufferers. We humbly conceive, that he who swears to more than he is certain of, is equally guilty of perjury with him that swears to what is false.'

They were so settled in their aversion, that they continued their persecutions for three or four years; and in July, 1697, they presented a remonstrance to arbitration, in which they accuse him of 'believing the devil's accusations, and readily departing from all charity to persons, though of blameless and godly lives, upon such suggestions against them; his promoting such accusations, as also his partiality in stifling the accusations of some, and vigilantly promoting others. His applying to those who have a familiar spirit to know who afflicted the people; which we consider as an implicit denying the providence of God, which alone we believe can send afflictions, or cause devils to afflict the people. By these practices and principles, Mr Parris hath been the beginner and procurer of the sorest afflictions, not to this village only, but this whole country, that did ever befall them.' Mr Parris did at length acknowledge his errors, but the people would not be satisfied till he was entirely dismissed.

At the period when the prosecutions for witchcraft were conducted at Salem, Sir William Phipps was governor of the Colony. He was a native of New England, of obscure origin, and very illiterate. His title and his affluence were acquired by fortuitous circumstances, not from any meritorious or honorable achievements. Mr Phipps had, by some means, obtained information that a Spanish ship loaded with gold and silver, had been wrecked on the coast of La Plata, many years before, and he resolved on a bold effort to possess himself of the booty. For the purpose of procuring assistance in the enterprise, he performed a voyage to England, where he obtained partners and associates, and from thence he proceeded to La Plata, in 1687. He was so fortunate as to discover the hulk, from which he recovered gold and silver to the amount of £300,000, his own share being £16,000. Having returned to England, and being introduced to men of rank and influence, he received from King James the Second, the honor of knighthood, and was commissioned as Governor of his native Colony. But, though a man of piety and integrity, he was not qualified to support the dignity of the office to which he had the honor of being promoted.

Sir William was a firm believer in witchcraft, and among the first acts of his authority, was an order for chaining the witches; stupidly believing that if the body was chained, the wicked spirit within could exert no power. But before the close of the tragedies, in which his excellency was so zealous an actor, his own wife, was by some of the complainants, accused of being a witch; but through favor to the governor's lady, she escaped without chains or halter.

It appears that Dr Cotton Mather was one of the leading champions in the persecution of witches. In October, 1692, at the desire of the governor, he published an account of the trials of seven of those who had been condemned and executed, in which he states that the court grounded their proceedings chiefly on the laws of England, and precedents found in books from thence. In his preface he has this passage. 'If in the midst of the many dissatisfactions among us, the publication of these trials may promote a pious thankfulness unto God for justice being so far executed among

An Essay on Demonology, Ghosts and Apparitions, and Popular Superstitions

us, I shall rejoice that God is glorified; and pray that no wrong steps of ours may ever sully any of his glorious works.' But it should be remembered that no condemnation can receive the sanction of justice nor the countenance of Christians, unless the party is fairly convicted by full and substantial human evidence. It is a most extraordinary circumstance that the rulers and judges, and the eminent divines of that day, should overlook the reasonable maxim in the Jewish constitution, that every word or thing admitted for evidence in the decision shall be established by the concurrence of what cometh from the mouth of two or three credible witnesses. 'So you will not pollute with blood the land in which you dwell.'--'And if a false witness rise up against a man, and accuse him of any crime, the two men before whom is the controversy, shall stand before the Lord, and before the priests, and before the judges, who may be in those days. And when the judges have made a strict examination, if the false witness hath testified falsehoods, and risen up against his brother; you shall do to him as he wickedly thought to do to his brother.'[C] It is melancholy to reflect that no instance can be found on record of a false witness against the innocent victims at Salem having been brought to merited punishment.

    Dr Mather, in his work entitled 'Wonders of the Invisible World,' produced an abridgment of the trials of the two women condemned by Lord Hale, 1664, and also an abridgment of the rules and signs by which witches are to be discovered, of which he says there are above thirty. His production received the approbation of two of the judges of the court, one of whom was the chief justice and lieutenant governor. The author's father, Dr Increase Mather, also expressed his coincidence in the same sentiments. The work is, nevertheless, a singular and curious production; it evinces, most clearly, that the reverend author, in the fervency of zeal, suffered his mind to be deeply imbued with bigotry and depressing superstition. Dr Mather was eminent for extensive knowledge and Christian piety; but foibles and infirmities were his lot, and while his mind was enriched with knowledge, his heart must have sickened for lack of wisdom. He published 382 books and tracts on various subjects. In these he displays wit and fancy, and advocates with zeal the cause of religion; and although his style is singular and verbose, his works contain rich and important matter for the historian and antiquary. It would be unjust not to acknowledge the debt of gratitude due to Dr Mather for the immeasurable benefits which our country and the world have enjoyed from his efforts to introduce smallpox inoculation, in 1721. But the work now in question affords a striking example of the imbecility of mind in the absence of its glorious attributes. Sobriety of judgment is seduced by folly, and moral dignity is degraded by the intrusion of fictions of imagination, and the man becomes a dupe to his own credulity. He adopted, in the fullest extent, the doctrine of demons, and of supernatural compacts between Satan and witches, and was fatally blinded against the most palpable impositions practised on himself. But this distinguished divine was not singular in his proneness to bigoted and dogmatical principles and doctrines; they were in perfect coincidence with the habits of thinking in the times in which he lived. His cotemporaries, who administered the affairs of government, and those who were called to decide in their judicial proceedings, had evidently imbibed the same gross absurdities; and there is in our nature an unaccountable reluctance to discard errors, however preposterous. His publication teems with romantic and ludicrous stories, which he unwisely adduces for substantial facts. A shrewd reply was made to it by R. Calef, a merchant of Boston, which led to a controversy between the two authors, on the subject of their inquiry.

    The following is an abridged narrative of the trials of B. Bishop, S. Martin, E. How, and M. Carryer, from Dr Mather's 'Wonders of the Invisible World.'

    'The court appeared to rely for evidence chiefly on the testimony of the accusers, and the incidents exhibited by the experiment with the parties in their presence on the trials. In all instances the presence of the accused would produce wonderful effects on the persons of the accusers. At a look, or cast of the eye, the accusers would instantly fall down as if in a fit or swoon, and would throw themselves into unnatural and painful postures, and by the application of the witches' hand they were immediately restored.[D] Some complained that the shape or spectre of B. Bishop, the prisoner on trial, pinched, choked, and bit them. One testified, that the shape of the prisoner, one day, took her from her wheel and carried her to the river side, threatening to drown her if she would not sign the devil's book, and said she had been the death of several persons whom she named. Another testified, that there were apparitions or ghosts seen with the spectre of the prisoner, crying out "You murdered us." There was testimony, likewise, that a man striking once at a place where a bewitched person said the shape of this Bishop stood, the bewitched cried out that he had torn her gown, and the woman's gown was found afterwards to be torn in the very place mentioned.

    'One D. Hobbs having confessed herself to be a witch was now tormented by the spectres for her confession, and this Bishop tempted her to sign the book again, and to deny what she had confessed, and it was the shape of this prisoner which whipped her with iron rods to compel her thereto. To render it further unquestionable, that the prisoner at the bar was the person truly charged in this witchcraft, there were produced many evidences of other witchcrafts by her perpetrated. J.

James Thacher, M. D., A. A. S.

Cook testified that, about five or six years ago, he was in his chamber assaulted by the shape of this prisoner, which looked on him, grinned at him, and very much hurt him with a blow on the side of his head; and on the same day about noon, the same shape walked into his room, and an apple strangely flew out of his hand into the lap of his mother, six or eight feet from him. S. Gray testified, that about fourteen years ago, he waked on a night and saw the room where he lay full of light, and saw plainly a woman between the cradle and the bed, which looked upon him. He rose, and it vanished, though the doors were all fast. He went to bed, and the same woman again assaulted him. The child in the cradle gave a great screech, and the woman disappeared. It was long before the child could be quieted; though it were a very likely, thriving child, yet from this time it pined away, and after divers months died in a sad condition. He was satisfied that it was the apparition of this Bishop which had thus troubled him. B. Coman testified, that eight years ago, as he lay awake in his bed with a light burning, he was annoyed with the apparition of this Bishop, and of two more, who came and oppressed him, that he could neither stir himself nor wake any one else; the said Bishop took him by the throat and pulled him almost out of bed. The next night his kinsman lodged with him, and as they were discoursing together, they were visited by the same guests, and the kinsman was struck speechless and unable to move hand or foot. He had laid his sword by him, which the spectres did strive much to wrest from him, but he held it too fast for them. S. Shattuck testified, that in the year 1680, this Bishop often came to his house on frivolous and foolish errands. Presently, whereupon, his eldest child began to droop exceedingly, and the oftener she came to his house the worse grew the child. He would be thrown and bruised against the stones by an invisible hand, and his face knocked against the sides of the house in a miserable manner, and the child's money, purse and all, would be unaccountably conveyed out of a locked box, and never seen more. The child was taken with terrible fits, and did nothing but cry and sleep for several months together, and at length his understanding was utterly taken away. Among other symptoms of enchantment upon him, one was, that there was a board in the garden whereon he would walk, and all the invitations in the world could never fetch him off. About seventeen or eighteen years after, there came a stranger to Shattuck's house, who, seeing the child, said this poor child is bewitched, and you have a neighbor who is a witch. J. Louder testified, that having some little controversy with Bishop about her fowls, he awaked in the night by moonlight, and clearly saw the likeness of this woman grievously oppressing him; she held him, unable to help himself, till near day. He told her of this, but she utterly denied it, and threatened him very much. Soon after this, being at home on a Lord's day, with the doors shut, he saw a black pig approach him, but it soon vanished away. Soon after he saw a black creature jump in at the window, and it came and stood before him. The body was like that of a monkey, the feet like a fowl's, but the face much like a man's. He was so extremely affrighted, that he could not speak; he endeavored to clap his hand upon it, but could feel no substance, and it jumped out of the window again. He struck at it, but missed his blow, and broke his stick; and the arm with which he struck was soon disabled. This same creature appeared again, and was going to fly at him, whereat he cried out, and it sprang back and flew over the apple tree, shaking many apples off the tree in flying over. At its leap it flung dirt with its feet against the stomach of the man, whereon he was then struck dumb, and so continued for three days. William Stacy testified, that having received some money of this Bishop for work done by him, he had gone but about three rods from her, when looking for his money it was unaccountably gone from him; and being about six rods from her, with a small load in his cart, suddenly the off wheel sunk down into a hole upon plain ground, so that he was forced to get help for the recovery of the wheel; but in searching for the hole in the ground, which might give him this disaster, there was none at all to be found. Soon after this, as he was in a dark night going to his barn, he was very suddenly lifted up from the ground and thrown against a stone wall; and after that he was again hoisted up and thrown down a bank. At another time this deponent passing by the said Bishop, his horse with a small load, striving to draw, all his gears flew to pieces, and the cart fell down, and the deponent going then to lift a bag of corn of about two bushels, could not lift it with all his might. Many other pranks of the prisoner this deponent was ready to testify. He verily believed that the said Bishop was the instrument of his daughter Priscilla's death. To crown all, says the Dr, J. Bly, and W. Bly, testified, that being employed by said Bishop to take down the cellar wall of the old house, wherein she formerly lived, they did, in holes of the said wall, find several puppets made up of rags and hogs' bristles, with headless pins in them, the points being outwards. Whereof she could now give no account unto the court, that was reasonable or tolerable. There might have been many more strange things brought against this woman, but there was no need of them. But there was one very strange thing more with which the court was entertained. As this woman was under guard, passing by the great and spacious meeting-house of Salem, she gave a look towards the house, and immediately a demon, invisibly entering the meeting-house, tore down a part of it; so that though there was no person to be seen there, yet the people at the noise, running in, found a board which was strongly fastened with several nails, transported into another quarter of the house.'

It will doubtless be conceded, that if Bridget Bishop was actually guilty of all the disasters above detailed, she was a proper subject for the gallows.

Footnotes:

A. Goodwife, Goody, and Goodman, were vulgar terms applied to heads of families by the lower class.

B. In an English court, a witness was about to relate an account of a murder as he received it from the ghost of the murdered person. 'Hold, sir,' said the judge; 'The ghost is an excellent witness, and his evidence the best possible, but he cannot be heard by proxy in this court; summon him hither, and I'll hear him in person; but your communication is mere hearsay, which my office compels me to reject.' If a court or magistrate will listen to ghost evidence to convict a reputed criminal, why not admit the same evidence on the contrary, in proof of innocence. And if a judge or magistrate countenance or abet such kind of juggling with diabolical influence, do they not come under the penalty of the statute of King James, which interdicts all acts of sorcery whatever, and all charms for employing spirits?

C. Numbers, xxxv. 30. Deut. xvii. 6, and xix. 15.

D. Why not bewitch the magistrates as well as others, and save the victims from death? If the witches, assisted by Satan, have power over the laws of nature and the actions of men, how is it that their enemies escape with impunity? If they possess the power of raising storms and sinking ships at sea, why not overwhelm both judge and jury in the ruins of falling houses and make a mock of the chains and ropes employed for their executions?

TRIAL OF SUSANNA MARTIN, JUNE 29, 1692.

Magistrate. 'Pray what ails these people?'
Martin. 'I don't know.'
Magistrate. 'But what do you think ails them?'
Martin. 'I do not desire to spend my judgment upon it.'
Magistrate. 'Don't you think they are bewitched?'
Martin. 'No, I do not think they are.'
Magistrate. 'Tell me your thoughts about them, then?'
Martin. 'No: my thoughts are my own, when they are in, but when they are out, then another's their master.'
Magistrate. 'Their master! who do you think is their master?'
Martin. 'If they be dealing in the black art you may know as well as I.'
Magistrate. 'Well, what have you done towards this?'
Martin. 'Nothing at all.'
Magistrate. 'Why, it is you or your appearance.'
Martin. 'I can't help it.'
Magistrate. 'Is it not your master? How comes your appearance to hurt these?'
Martin. 'How do I know? He that appeared in the shape of Samuel, a glorified saint, may appear in any one's shape.'

It was then also noted, that if the afflicted went to approach her, they were flung down to the ground. The court counted themselves alarmed by these things, to inquire farther into the conversation of the prisoner, and see what might occur to render these accusations further credible. John Allen testified, that he refused, because of the weakness of his oxen, to cart some stones, at the request of this Martin. She was displeased, and said it had been as good that he had, for his oxen should never do him any more service. Whereupon, as he was going home, one of his oxen tired, so that he was forced to unyoke him that he might get him home. He put his oxen, with many others, on Salisbury beach; they all ran into Merrimack river, and the next day were found on Plum Island. They next ran, with a violence that seemed wholly diabolical, right into the sea, swimming as far as they could be seen; and out of fourteen good oxen all were drowned, save one. John Atkinson testified, that he exchanged a cow with the son of said Martin, whereat she muttered and was unwilling he should have it. Going to receive his cow, though he hamstringed her, and haltered her, she, of a tame creature, grew so mad they could scarce get her along. She broke all the ropes that were fastened unto her, and, though she was tied fast to a tree, yet she made her escape, and gave them such further trouble, as they could ascribe it to no cause but witchcraft. J. Kemball testified, that the said Martin, upon a causeless disgust, threatened him that a certain cow should never do him any more service, and it came to pass accordingly, for soon after the cow was found stark dead on the ground, without any distemper to be discerned upon her; and this was followed with the death of several more of his cattle. 'But,' says the reverend author, 'the said J. Kemball had a further testimony against the prisoner, which was truly admirable. He applied himself to buy a dog of this Martin; but she, not letting him have his choice, he said he would supply himself at one Blazdel's, and marked a puppy there which he liked. G. Martin, the husband of the prisoner, asked him if he would not have one of his wife's puppies, and he answered, no. Whereupon the prisoner replied, "As I live I will give him puppies enough." Within a few days after, Kemball coming out of the woods, there arose a little black cloud in the N. W. and Kemball immediately felt a force upon him, which made him not able to avoid running upon the stumps of trees, although he had a broad, plain, cart way before him; but though he had his axe on his shoulder to endanger him in his falling, he could not forbear going out of his way to tumble over them. When he came below the meeting-house, there appeared to him a little creature like a puppy, of a darkish color, and it shot backwards and forwards between his legs. He had the courage to use all possible endeavors to cut it with his axe, but he could not hit it, the puppy gave a jump from him, and went, as to him it seemed, into the ground. On going a little further, there appeared unto him a black puppy, bigger than the first, but as black as a Coal. Its motions were quicker than those of his axe. It flew at him and at his throat over his shoulders one way, and then over his shoulders another way; his heart now began to fail him, and he thought the dog would have tore his throat out. But he recovered himself and called on God in his distress, and it vanished away at once.'--'This S. Martin once walked from Amesbury to Newbury in an extraordinary season, when it was not fit for any one to travel. She bragged and showed how dry she was; it could not be perceived that so much as the soles of her shoes were wet. Being told that another person would have been wet up to the knees, she replied, "she scorned to be drabbled." It was noted that this testimony upon her trial, cast her into a very singular confusion. John Pressy testified, that being one evening bewildered near the field of Martin, as under enchantment, he saw a marvellous light, about the bigness of a half bushel, near two rods out of the way. He struck at it with a stick and laid it on with all his might. He gave it near forty blows and felt it a palpable substance. But going from it, his heels were struck up, and he was laid with his back on the ground, sliding, as he thought, into a pit, from whence he recovered by taking hold on the bush, although afterwards he could find no pit in the place. Having gone five or six rods he saw S. Martin standing on his left hand, as the light had done before, but they changed no words with one another. At length he got home extremely affrighted. The next day it was upon inquiry understood, that Martin was in a miserable condition by pains and hurts that were upon her.' (Forty stout blows would have killed any one but a witch.) 'The deponent further testified, that having affronted the prisoner, many years ago, she said he should never prosper; more particularly, that he should never have more than two cows; that though he were ever so likely to have more than two cows, yet he should never have them. From that very day to this, namely, for twenty years together, he could never exceed that number, but some strange thing or other still prevented his having more.'

TRIAL OF ELIZABETH HOW, JUNE 30, 1692.

'The most remarkable things ascribed to E. How, were, that the sufferers complained of her as the cause of their distresses, and they would fall down when she looked on them and were raised again on the touch of her hand. There was testimony, also, that the shape of her gave trouble to people nine or ten years ago. There were apparitions or ghosts testified by some of the present sufferers, which ghosts affirmed that this How had murdered them. J. How, brother to the husband of the prisoner, testified, that having refused to accompany her to her examination, as she desired, immediately some of his cattle were bewitched to death, leaping three or four feet high, squeaking, falling, and dying at once; and going to cut off an ear, the hand wherein the knife was held, was taken very numb and painful, and so remained for several days, and he suspected the prisoner as the cause of it. N. Abbot testified, that unusual and mischievous accidents would befall his cattle whenever he had any difference with her. Once in particular, he wished his ox choked, and within a little while that ox was choked with a turnip in his throat. A woman, on some difference with How, was bewitched, and she died charging her of having a hand in her death. Many people had their barrels of beer unaccountably mischiefed, spoiled, and spilt, upon displeasing her. One testified, that they once and again lost great quantities of drink out of their vessels, in such a manner as they could ascribe it to nothing but witchcraft. And also that How once gave her some apples, and when she had eaten them, she was taken with a very strange kind of maze, so that she knew not what she said or did. There was likewise a cluster of depositions that one J. Cummings refused to lend his mare to the husband of the said How; the mare was within a day or two taken in a strange condition. She seemed abused and bruised as if she had been running over the rocks, and was marked where the bridle went, as if burnt with a red hot bridle. On using a pipe of tobacco for the cure of the beast, a blue flame issued out of her which took hold of her hair and not only spread and burnt on her, but it also flew upwards towards the roof of the barn and like to have set the barn on fire, and the mare died very suddenly. F. Lane being hired by the husband of How to get him a parcel of posts and rails, Lane hired J. Pearly to assist him. The prisoner told Lane that the posts and rails would not do because Pearly helped him, but if he had gotten them alone they might have done well enough. When How came to receive his posts and rails, on taking them up by the ends, they, though good and sound, yet unaccountably broke off, so that Lane had to get twenty or thirty more. And this prisoner being informed of it, said she told him so before, because Pearly helped about them.'

TRIAL OF MARTHA CARRYER, AUGUST 2, 1692.

A considerable number of bewitched persons deposed that it was Martha Carryer or her shape, that grievously tormented them by biting, pricking, pinching, and choking them; the poor people were so tortured, that every one expected their death upon the very spot, but that on the binding of the prisoner they were eased. Moreover, the looks of Carryer then laid the afflicted people for dead; and her touch, if her eyes at the same time were off them, raised them again. It was testified, that on the mention of some having their necks twisted almost round by the shape of this Carryer, she replied, it's no matter though their necks had been twisted quite off. B. Abbot testified, that the prisoner was very angry with him upon laying out some land near her husband's. She was heard to say she would hold Abbot's nose as close to the grindstone as ever it was held since his name was Abbot. Presently after this, he was taken with a swelling in his foot, and then with a pain in his side, and exceedingly tormented. It bred a sore which was lanced by Dr Prescott. For six weeks it continued very bad, and then another sore bred, and finally a third, all which put him to very great misery. He was brought to death's door, and so remained till Carryer was taken and carried away by the constable. From which very day he began to mend and so grew better every day. Abbot was not only afflicted in his body but suffered greatly in the loss of his cattle in a strange and unaccountable manner. One A. Toothaker testified, that Richard, the son of M. Carryer, having some difference with him, pulled him down by the hair of his head; when he rose again he was going to strike at Richard, but fell down flat on his back to the ground, and had not power to stir hand or foot until he told Carryer he yielded, and then he saw the shape of his mother, the prisoner, go off his breast. One Foster, who had confessed herself a witch, testified, that she had seen the prisoner at some of their witch meetings, and that the devil carried them on a pole, but the pole broke and she hanging about Carryer's neck, they both fell down and she received a hurt by the fall. Many other evidences of her mischievous conduct were produced, which I omit; the last was this. In the time of the prisoner's trial, one S. Sheldon, in open court, had her hands unaccountably tied together with a wheel band, so fast, that without cutting, it could not be loosened. It was done, says Dr Mather, by a spectre, and the sufferer affirmed it was the prisoner's.

***

There is something in the foregoing proceedings during the memorable events at Salem, that seems to surpass all our conceptions of impartial justice, christian charity, or humanity. It is humiliating to our nature to reflect, that a class of the most profligate wretches were brought together on the stage, and their base intrigues tolerated and encouraged, fanciful experiments witnessed, and little else than fictitious evidence of accusation received to condemnation; while all pleadings for mercy, on the score of innocence, were of no avail. Not a solitary instance is found on record of the voice of pity and compassion being raised in behalf of the friendless, ignorant victims of suspicion. They were subjected to barbarous tricks and senseless experiments, calculated to encourage fraud and imposition, and then consigned to the gallows for the consequences. Better that ten guilty persons escape, than one innocent should suffer. Unfortunately, no lawyers were at that time employed in criminal cases. Had our present court and our state prison been then in existence, the good people of Salem would not long have been molested by witches and bewitched girls, with their invisible ropes and chains.

But while we contemplate the melancholy errors of judgment in our predecessors, we ought in charity to cherish the belief that had not their minds been clouded in superstitious darkness, their posterity would not have been called to mourn over imbecilities so lamentably exemplified. But we would attribute to our venerated fathers no moral corruption, no perverseness of temper, no desire to swerve from the dictates of stern justice. Their task was most arduous, their path of duty obscured by novel occurrences, and their decisions unavoidably swayed by popular clamor and vulgar prejudice. If, unhappily, their intellects were tinctured with superstition, it was the effect of early education, fostered and confirmed by concurrent sentiment and opinion, propagated in books of the heathen and papist.

Much importance was attached by the magistrates to the effects of the witches' eyes upon the sufferers; but no explanation is given why the same eyes could produce no mischievous effects on any other person. Great stress was laid on the circumstance, that in the trials the sufferers were revived from their fits by the touch of the hand of the reputed witch, but not by the hand of any other person; but instances of the contrary can be adduced; the experiment was ordered to be made in a court in England; the afflicted girl's eyes being blindfolded, and she being touched by the hand of another woman, recovered as speedily as if touched by the accused witch.

The Rev. Dr Increase Mather, then President of Harvard College, may be considered as among the best authorities for the prevalent doctrines on the subject of witchcraft. On the 19th of October, 1692, he went to Salem and conferred with eight of the confessing witches, all of whom freely and relentlessly recanted their former confessions, declaring that in making them they had violated the truth, being compelled to it by pressing threats and urgings, by which they were so affrighted as to agree to anything that would rescue them from their awful situation. But they confessed with anguish of soul that they had committed a great wickedness for which they implored forgiveness. In his 'Cases of Conscience,' published in 1693, Dr Mather has particular reference to the trials at Salem. In this work he observes, that 'the gift of healing the sick and possessed, was a special grace and favor of God for the confirmation of the truth of the gospel, but that such a gift should be annexed to the touch of wicked witches, as an infallible sign of their guilt is not easy to be believed.' If it be as supposed, by virtue of some compact with the devil, that witches have power to do such things, those who encourage them in the practice, whether courts or individuals, must be guilty of sacrilege. The accusers pretended to suffer much by bites, and the prints on the skin would compare precisely with the set of teeth of the accused, but those who had not such bewitched eyes, have seen the accusers bite themselves and then complain of the accused. It was true, also, that some who complained of being pricked by pins sticking in their flesh, were their own tormentors, for the purpose of effecting their wicked designs. The pins thus employed are still preserved at Salem. Dr Mather, in the work just quoted, judiciously affirms, that the evidence in the crime of witchcraft ought to be as clear as in any other crimes of a capital nature. He is decidedly opposed to the employment of spectral evidence as being alone sufficient to justify conviction. But he considers a free and voluntary confession as a sufficient ground of conviction; yet the reverend author himself cites one remarkable instance of false confession for the avowed purpose of effecting her own death in consequence of the cruel persecution which she suffered from suspicion only, and she was burnt at the stake. In most of the instances at Salem, the confessions proved false and deceptive, those who made them being totally ignorant of the nature of witchcraft. Our learned author further observes, that if two credible persons shall affirm on oath that they have seen the person accused, doing things which none but such as have familiarity with the devil ever did or can do, that is a sufficient ground of conviction. It was on this ground that he justified the condemnation and execution of George Burroughs, the minister; it being testified before the court, that he had been seen to lift a barrel of molasses or cider, and to extend with one hand a heavy musket at arms' length. Nothing could be more sophistical than evidence of this description, for there are persons who can lift a solid body of six or seven hundred pounds, and can extend a king's arm at arms' length, when held at the smallest end with one hand, and no jury in our day would condemn such to the gallows as wizards.

It is among the most unaccountable facts, that those who, to save their lives, belied their consciences, and confessed themselves guilty of having formed a league with the devil, and of committing horrid crimes, should be spared and suffered to live in society, while others, relying on their innocence, honestly despised those tempting conditions, should be consigned to the gallows. In fact, false confessions, fraud, and counterfeit, were so palpable, that the halter might with more justice have been applied to the accusers than to those who actually suffered.

But such, at that time, was the state of the public mind, that the more extravagant the tale, the more implicitly was it regarded. The hostility to witchcraft was so prevalent as to give a general bias unfriendly to the fair development of truth, or to the impartial examination of facts and circumstances. The unhappy victims were without defence, and their total ignorance subjected them to the most cruel treatment and sufferings. In one instance on record, there appears to us to be a profanation of the Lord's Prayer. The woman being required to repeat it before the court, instead of 'deliver us from evil,' expressed it 'deliver us from all evil;' this was considered as referring to her own condition, and she was ordered to repeat it again. On the second trial, instead of 'hallowed be thy name,' she expressed 'hollowed be thy name.' Thus by her using the o, in place of a, it was concluded that she could not say the Lord's Prayer, and she was committed to jail as a witch.

In Dr Mather's 'Magnalia,' we have the following instance of witchcraft.

In the year 1679, the house of William Morse, at Newbury, was infested with demons. 'Bricks, and sticks, and stones, were often by some invisible hand, thrown at the house, and so were many pieces of wood; a cat was thrown at the woman of the house, and a long staff was danced up and down in the chimney, and afterwards the same long staff was hanged by a line, and swung to and fro, and when two persons laid it on the fire to burn, it was as much as they were able to do with their joint strength to hold it there. An iron crook was violently, by an invisible hand, hurled about, and a chair flew about the room until at last it lit upon the table, where the food stood ready to be eaten, and would have spoiled all, if the people had not with much ado saved a little. A chest, was by an invisible hand, carried from one place to another, and the doors barricaded; and the keys of the family taken some of them from the bunch where they were tied, and the rest flying about with a loud noise. For a while the people of the house could not sup quietly; ashes would be thrown into their suppers and on their heads. The man's shoes being left below, one of them would be filled with ashes and coals and thrown up after him. When in bed a stone, weighing about three pounds, was divers times thrown upon them. A box and a board were likewise thrown upon them, and a bag of hops being taken out of a chest, they were by the invisible hand, beaten therewith, till some of the hops were scattered on the floor, where the bag was then laid and left. The man was often struck by that hand, with several instruments, and the same hand cast their good things into the fire; yea, while the man was at prayer, a broom gave him a blow on his head behind and fell down before his face. While the man was writing, his ink-stand was by the invisible hand snatched from him, and being able nowhere to find it, he saw it at length drop out of the air down by the fire. A shoe was laid on his shoulder, and when he would have catched it, it was snatched from him and was then clapped on his head, and there held so fast, that the unseen fury pulled him with it backward on the floor. He had his cap torn off his head, and in the night he was pulled by the hair and pinched, and scratched; and the invisible hand pricked him with some of his awls, and with needles, and bodkins, and blows that fetched blood were sometimes given him. His wife going down into the cellar, the trap door was immediately by an invisible hand shut upon her, and a table brought and laid upon the door. When he was writing another time, a dish went and leaped into a pail and cast water upon the man and spoiled what he was about. His cap jumped off his head and on again, and the pot lid went off the pot into the kettle, then over the fire together. A little boy belonging to the family was a principal sufferer, for he was flung about at such a rate, that it was feared his brains would be beaten out. His bed-clothes would be pulled from him, his bed shaken, leaping forward and backward. The man took him to hold in a chair, but the chair fell a dancing, and both of them were very near being thrown into the fire. These, and a thousand such vexations, befalling the boy at home, they carried him to live at a doctor's. There he was quiet, but returning home he suddenly cried out he was pricked on the back, where was found strangely sticking a three tined fork belonging to the doctor, and had been seen at his house after the boy's departure. Afterwards his troublers found him out at the doctor's also, when crying out again he was pinched on the back, they found an iron spindle stuck into him; and on the like outcry again, they found pins in a paper stuck into him, and a long iron, a bowl of a spoon stuck upon him. He was taken out of his bed and thrown under it, and all the knives in the house were one after another stuck into his back; which the spectators pulled out, only one of them seemed to the spectators to come out of his mouth. The spectre would make all his meat, when he was going to eat, fly out of his mouth, and instead thereof make him fall to eating ashes, sticks, and yarn.'

The foregoing has all the air of an exaggerated narrative, and it is probable that Dr Mather, in his love for the marvellous and wonderful, recorded the circumstances without due examination, but merely from the uncertain rumor among the credulous neighbors. The same story is found on the records of the court at Salem, but with the following explanatory circumstances as I have received them. It so happened, that one Caleb Powell, an intelligent seaman, suspected that a boy, the grandson of Morse, who lived in the family, was the cause of all the mischief, and watched for an opportunity of detecting him. Going one morning to Morse's house, he saw through the window, the said boy throw a shoe slyly at the old man's head. Upon this, Powell told Morse that if he would let his boy come and live with him a short time, he guessed that with a little astrology and a little astronomy, he could unravel the mystery. Morse reluctantly consented, and his house was not molested during the boy's absence. This, Morse acknowledged, but yet, unwilling to suspect the boy, he and his neighbors concluded that Powell had studied the black art, and had by that means been the cause of all the mischief about Morse's house. Powell was accordingly apprehended and tried at Salem. The testimony against him was singular. One testified, that he had heard him say that by a little astrology and a little astronomy, he guessed he could find out the cause of Morse's trouble. Another testified, that he heard it said that Powell had studied the black art with one Norwood, a famous magician beyond sea. The result of the trial was, that although they could find no positive evidence of his guilt, yet he had given so much ground for suspicion, that he deserved to bear his own shame and the costs of court. Morse's wife was at another time tried for witchcraft, and condemned to be hung, but was afterwards reprieved, and died a pious woman.

The following is an amusing story, well told, but it is from newspaper authority, the Galaxy. About the year 1760, the fury of the inhabitants of New England had declined towards suspected old women, but their believing fear was not altogether quelled. At this time, a case of witchcraft occurred in Billerica, under the ministry of the Rev. Dr Cummings, who related the story with much satisfaction, as the last which came within his precincts.

An old woman, of very peaceable character, lived pretty much alone in a shell of a house near

James Thacher, M. D., A. A. S.

the meeting-house and the clergyman's dwelling. She was suspected of witchcraft by a family who lived at two miles' distance, in the west part of the town, and they brought accusation immediately to the parson; who in those early times, exercised not only the spiritual, but the temporal power of the parish; he was often counsel for both parties, and was judge and jury, without subjection to appeal. He was, moreover, a peace-maker. Mr C. accused Mrs D. of witchcraft. 'How do you know she is a witch?' 'Because she has bewitched my mare.' 'How do you know that your mare is bewitched?' 'Because she won't stand still to be saddled, and the minute I get on, she kicks up and throws me off.' 'But what makes you think that Mrs D. has bewitched her?' No answer. 'Have you had a quarrel with her?' 'Oh no! I have had no quarrel.' 'But what is the matter? surely she would not bewitch her for nothing.' 'Why I carried her some corn on the mare about a week ago, and I didn't know but I might have made a mistake in the measure so that it fell short, and so'--'And because your corn fell short, you suspect that she found it out, and is so angry as to bewitch your mare.' 'Yes, that's it, and I want you to go and lay the devil.' 'Why, if you have raised the devil by cheating in the corn, you had better lay him yourself.' 'Yes, but I don't know how.' 'Go then, directly, and carry the balance of the corn, and take good care never to commit such an act again: the devil is always busy with people who do not perform all their duties honestly.' The man slunk away home at this unexpected rebuke, and failed not to carry corn enough to make full measure; which, however, he feared to carry into the house to the old woman, but emptied it down upon the door-stone. But the mare ceased to kick as usual; whereupon Mr C. came to the minister, told him what he had done, and begged for holy assistance. 'Go home,' said the parson, with all that energy for which he was so remarkable, 'go home,--you need not trouble yourself about witches; I'll not allow them to do any mischief, I assure you--do your duty, so as to escape a guilty conscience, and if your mare is refractory, whip her, as I do mine--go, and let me hear no more about witches.' Mr C. obeyed, but he was far from convinced that Mrs D. was not a witch, and he determined to put it to the proof. For this purpose he boiled a large potato, which he put directly from the boiling water, under the bewitched mare's saddle. The caperings and kickings of the poor beast were excusable this time, at least, for when after some hours the saddle was got off, it was found that a severe mark was left behind it. The proof of the matter was to be this; if the old woman had bewitched the mare, she would have the same mark of a burn on her back. Two old women were prevailed on to be of the examining committee. Dr Cummings was requested to be of the party, with his Bible at hand, to prevent any fatal explosion from Satan's nostrils. This office he prudently declined. His place was supplied by another old woman, and Saturday night was appointed for this examination. This time was chosen, because the good people thought that Satan would not visit in holy hours. In the meantime, the good woman got an inkling of what was going on; and as they entered a long dark entry, they were saluted with a stupendous flash of powder and tow, and a glorious clatter of tin pans. The committee was scattered of course--and before church the next day, everybody in the town knew, that the devil came, all covered with blue brimstone, to save his disciple, the wicked Mrs D. This would have made a new era in witchcraft in the town, but for the pertinent remarks of the parson touching the matter; for he was enabled to dispense a word in season.

It is but a few years since, a farmer at Kennebunk, observing his cattle to be affected with some fatal disease, conceived the idea that they were bewitched, and fixed his suspicion on a poor widow who had become insane in consequence of the death of her husband at sea. He was so confident of her guilt, that he went to her lonely cottage, and with his ox goad, beat and abused her in a cruel manner. It is not under our salutary laws that a crime so atrocious can pass with impunity. The culprit was prosecuted and received the merited punishment.

The family of M'Farlain, of Pembroke, were remarkable for peculiarity of character and manners. About the year 1789, Seth M'Farlain attracted the notice of the neighborhood by being supposed to be under the influence of witchcraft. He became an object of wonder and commiseration to some, and of curiosity and ridicule to others. Hundreds of people thronged round his house from time to time, gazing with astonishment at his supposed personal sufferings; inflicted, as he pretended, by a certain old hag in the neighborhood. He was desired to visit the woman at her house, but before he could reach the door, his limbs would fail him, and he would fall to the ground. His body was occasionally distorted and convulsed, he would utter the bitterest complaints of pain and distress, which he ascribed to the presence of the hag, although she was invisible to all but himself. He consulted Judge T--r, to know whether he would be culpable in law if he should kill a witch. The Judge observing Seth on the bed with a club, swinging his arms to and fro, to keep off the witch, was willing to humor the whim, and procured a gun, and loading it with some pieces of silver, enjoined on Seth to take a sure aim when the witch again made her appearance. Accordingly, Seth pointed the gun to the door where she usually entered, and hung up her bonnet, and at the proper time he discharged his piece. The discharge shattered the door in pieces, but the cunning witch dodged her head at the moment he pulled the trigger!

James Thacher, M. D., A. A. S.

OMENS AND AUGURIES

In ancient times, especially among the Greeks and Romans, omens and auguries were considered as of great importance in the common concerns of life; but having their origin in ignorance and superstition, they vanished before the light of philosophy and wisdom. But so late as the first part of the last century, the belief in fairies, hobgoblins, witches, and omens, prevailed almost universally among the superstitious part of the community; and even some of superior rank and condition in life, were under the influence of these chimerical fancies.

The following were among the lucky and unlucky omens.

The flight of singing birds, or the manner of feeding of birds and chickens, portended good or evil, according to particular circumstances. The act of sneezing was ominous of good or evil, according to the number at the time, or the place. If, when a servant is making a bed, she happens to sneeze, no person can sleep in it undisturbed, unless a part of the straw or feathers be taken out and burnt. Nothing could insure success to a person going on important business, more effectually than to throw an old shoe after him on leaving the house. If there be in company thirteen persons, the devil's dozen, some misfortune will befall one of them. To spill salt, at table, is very ominous, and the ticking of the small insect called a death-watch, foretels death, and the screech-owl at midnight, some terrible misfortune. These, and many other silly fancies, have been keenly satirized by Addison, in the Spectator. To find a horse-shoe was deemed lucky, more especially, if it be preserved and nailed on the door, as this prevents the annoyance of witches. This, probably, was the origin of the practice continued in our times, of nailing horse shoes on the masts of vessels, against the enchantment of witches. The omens are extended to particular days in the week. Friday, for instance, is considered an inauspicious day for the commencement of any undertaking. It is seldom that a seaman can be prevailed on to commence a voyage on that day. An account has been published of some person, who, desirous of eradicating this prejudice, ordered the timber of his vessel to be cut on Friday; her foundation laid, her launching, and the engaging her crew, on Friday, and finally he ordered her to sail on Friday. But it was remarkable and unfortunate, that neither the vessel nor crew were ever heard from afterwards. This, however, is no proof that Friday is more likely to produce disasters than any other day in the seven. We know that all events are under the control of Divine Providence, and it is inconsistent with reason to imagine, that fatality will attend undertakings because they were commenced on any one particular day.

That singular genius, Lord Byron, was among those who indulged the superstitious notion, that Friday is an unlucky day. In Moore's Life of Byron, may be found the following.

'Among the superstitions in which he chose to indulge, the supposed unluckiness of Friday, as a day for the commencement of any work, was one by which he almost always allowed himself to be influenced. Soon after his arrival at Pisa, a lady of his acquaintance happening to meet him on the road from her house, as she was herself returning thither, and supposing that he had been to make her a visit, requested that he would go back with her. "I have not been to your house," he answered; "for just before I got to the door I remembered that it was Friday; and not liking to make my first visit on a Friday, I turned back." It is even related of him, that he once sent away a Genoese tailor, who brought him home a new coat on the same ominous day. With all this, strange to say, he set sail for Greece on a Friday; and, though by those who have any leaning to this superstitious fancy, the result may be thought but too sadly confirmatory of the omen, it is plain, that either the influence of superstition over his own mind was slight, or, in the excitement of self devotion under which he now acted, was forgotten.'

In Lord Byron, we have an example of the fatal consequences which sometimes ensue from prejudices against any particular purpose or object, being instilled into the youthful mind. Of all his prejudices, he declared the strongest was that against bleeding. His mother had on her death bed obtained from him a promise never to consent to being bled. When on his own death bed, therefore, he pertinaciously opposed the operation, contrary to the united and earnest entreaties of his physicians, and it was delayed till too late to afford him the desired relief.

History furnishes one signal instance of a successful enterprise commenced on Friday. It was on that day that Christopher Columbus sailed from the port of Palos on his first voyage of discovery; and it was on Friday that he landed on an island never before seen by European eyes. Of

An Essay on Demonology, Ghosts and Apparitions, and Popular Superstitions
all events recorded in modern history, this is incomparably the most important.

A curious and melancholy instance of aberration of intellect, occurred on board the ship President, on her outward bound passage to Charleston. She encountered very heavy weather, and one of the sailors stated to his shipmates that he was convinced the storm had arisen entirely in consequence of his wicked course of life, and that the offended majesty of heaven could only be appeased by his immediately precipitating himself into the sea. In vain was every argument urged, and every endeavor made, on the part of the captain and his officers, to induce him to relinquish his purpose. One evening he ascended the main rigging, and putting off a part of his attire, threw himself headlong into the deep. When the ship was returning to this city, a storm of considerable violence arose, which called forth all the superstition of the mariners, and a cry became universal that she would go down unless 'Sam's' chest was thrown overboard. A Scotchman was among the most bigoted portion of the crew, and having more dread of the elements than the captain, he, by some means or other, procured the chest of poor 'Sam,' and entombed it in the grave of its owner. The storm almost immediately abated; calmness reigned upon the face of the waters, and a fine breeze wafted them to the mouth of the harbor. Here, however, the wind became unpropitious, and a squall from the land drove them off. Discontent again manifested its influence, and a general search took place to ascertain whether anything belonging to the suicide remained. After the forecastle had been duly searched, an old shoe was discovered, and hastily yielded up as a sacrifice to Eolus. The wind again subsided, and a fair breeze brought them into port; the whole scene without doubt, confirming their minds in the superstition they had cherished.--N. Y. J. of Commerce.

On board of a ship, Capt V. master, it became necessary in the night, to reef the topsails; the sails were lowered, and the reef tackle hauled out, when the sailors ascended the mast; but to the surprise of the captain, they soon came down in great terror, crying out that the devil was in the top, they knew him by his horns, flashing eyes, and grisly beard. No commands or threats from the captain could avail, to induce them to make another attempt. All other orders they were willing to obey, but to encounter the devil on the topmast was too much. The affair began to grow serious, for the topsail was quivering and shivering in the wind. The captain and officers resolved with courage to ascend, but they, too, were driven in terror to the deck. It was now agreed, be their fate what it may, to wait till the morning; when by daylight it was discovered, that an old goat was seated on the top, with its glaring eyes staring the seamen in the face. It appeared that the goat was sleeping on the halliards while coiled in a tub, and was by that means hoisted up to the top without the knowledge of any one.

The Roman Catholics have been educated in the full persuasion that the devil appears in bodily form, and often in the high style of some great personage. I have more than once listened to an honest Irish Catholic while gravely relating the manner in which Satan appeared on horseback with a splendid retinue, and took possession of a gentleman's palace in Ireland, after the massacre of the Romish priests. His majesty having taken possession of the palace, a Protestant minister was sent to drive him to his own abode, but he was received with a laugh and sneer, as possessing no power. But at length a Catholic priest, who had been secreted in a cavern during the massacre, was sent, and he no sooner entered than the devil in a fright, flew up the chimney, carrying an iron pot from over the fire, and in passing out carrying off the top of the chimney. The Irishman entertained not the least doubt of the reality of the transaction; and added that the chimney still remains in the same state, no one daring to mend it.

Some old seamen admire to be considered as being on familiar terms with the devil. The following story has often been related by sailors in the full belief of its truth.

A sailor sold himself to the devil, on condition that he should enjoy all the good things and pleasures of this life for fifty years, when he would give himself up; but the devil was to perform any one thing which the sailor might desire before he surrendered. At the expiration of fifty years, Satan came for his man. The sailor acknowledged that the time had expired, but one thing was to be done. Satan was required to pump the sea dry, but the cunning son of Neptune had so placed the pump that the water from it flowed directly into the sea again. The devil was so enraged at this cunning artifice, that he gave him a tremendous blow with his tail and vanished in a cloud of smoke and brimstone.

The Reformation of the 16th century, although it in a great measure broke the shackles which bound the human intellect, and taught men to think, did not altogether eradicate heathen and popish absurdities, even from the reformers themselves. What, but a spirit of bigotry, could influence the great mind of Martin Luther gravely to declare that he experienced several personal encounters with the devil, in consequence of his being engaged in reforming the abuses of the Catholic Church, and particularly that his 'Satanic majesty entered his bolted chamber one night, stole his hazel nuts, and cracked them on his bed-post, to his no small annoyance?'

The Rev. Mr Whitman, in his ingenious lecture on Popular Superstition, relates, that 'Not

James Thacher, M. D., A. A. S.

many years ago, a man was suddenly missing from a certain town in this commonwealth. The church immediately sent one of her members to consult the far-famed fortune-teller, Molly Pitcher. After making the necessary inquiries, she intimated that the absent person had been murdered by a family of negroes, and his body sunk in the deep waters behind their dwelling. Upon this evidence, the accused were forthwith imprisoned, and the pond raked in vain from shore to shore. A few days previous to the trial, the murdered man returned to his friends safe and sound.' The church would have done themselves more credit, had they taken the legal means for the punishment of the fortune-teller in the penitentiary for defamation.

I cannot omit to communicate the following excellent remarks in the language of my amiable and learned friend and correspondent, Thomas Miner, M. D. of Middletown, Conn.

'That demons could ever work miracles, seems to be incredible; but mind as well as matter was evidently subject to different laws anciently, from what they are at present. This principle may perhaps help to a satisfactory solution of many things otherwise involved in inextricable perplexity in the Scriptures. God never violated, and can never violate, known laws, but he can change them at pleasure. Every geologist knows he has changed them since the creation, for by no law now existing, can we account for the organic remains of tropical animals, and plants in arctic and temperate regions. There have, therefore, been miracles, or variations, or suspensions, or additions, to the common laws of nature, as respects the physical world. Science teaches this, particularly geology, and this cuts, or rather unties, the gordian knot in the material world. The analogy is complete in the world of mind; at least, revelation informs us that the ordinary laws of mind, and of matter too, have been occasionally varied, suspended, or have had supplementary additions, as is the fact in all the miracles recorded in Scripture. If Hume had only been a modern geologist, he would have seen the futility of his reasoning against the possibility of miracles, for he would have had facts staring him in the face, demonstrating that matter had at times been governed by laws very different in kind or in degree, or in both, from any that are now known to exist. Analogy shows that this may have been the case with mind; Scripture says it has been.

'I must confess, I am very cautious in explaining away a single miraculous event recorded in the Scriptures, since if I begin I know not where to stop; but if I only admit this principle, that though the general laws of matter and mind have always been the same, yet the Creator has frequently, for great and wise purposes, deviated from them himself, and permitted, or authorized, or empowered others, sometimes, on important occasions, to deviate from them, (as we know has been the fact in the material world) nearly every difficulty in the interpretation of the marvellous part of revelation, at once becomes of easy solution. Perhaps it may be objected that this does not solve the difficulty concerning the miraculous agency of bad men or other depraved beings. But revelation does mention cases of bad men prophesying, working miracles, and performing other wonders, whom the Saviour never knew. True science, wherever it is properly applied, must destroy superstition and fanaticism, but as is the case with geology, showing that miracles or changes of the laws of nature have existed, it serves to support real religion, and demonstrates the immoveable basis on which it is founded. Philosophy shows that miracles have existed, revelation records the time, place, and occasion. After all, I would speak with great caution concerning the ancient demoniacs, whatever side of the question we take, much remains that is mysterious and perhaps incomprehensible by our present imperfect faculties.

'In most points of view, we live in the best age the world ever saw; but we live in an age of excitement. Every, almost every project, is begun and pursued with enthusiasm. The difficulty is to keep from running into complete fanaticism. Mere duty or expediency, however, is a cold thing, and never alone does much, unless it is attended with some zeal, some ardor, some earnestness of feeling. These latter emotions should resemble the steady, but gentle breeze; but passion, especially, when protracted into fanaticism, is like the hurricane and tornado. I know of no way to insure the golden mean with any prospect of success, except by giving the rising generation a stable education, founded upon the sure basis of the morality and religion of the gospel. The sermon on the mount contains the best rules of duty, and the thirteenth chapter of the first Corinthians, the best exposition of them, anywhere to be found. The great law of love, enforcing a disposition to do to others as we would wish them to do to us, is practically exemplified in the charity which is so much insisted on by Paul.'

It is incumbent upon us as patriots and philanthropists, as far as in our power, to guard the rising generation against every species of superstition, by a strong bulwark laid deep and early in the minds of our children. It is our children that are to be entrusted with our character, our acquirements, and our sentiments; whether fraught with pure wisdom, or tinctured with brain-sick infirmities, future generations will know how to appreciate their worth. If we wish posterity to enjoy true and permanent happiness, let them be taught to cultivate their intellectual powers, and fortify their minds against deceptive illusions and imaginary evils. Spectral illusions may be experienced while the intellectual faculties remain entire, as is exemplified in the cases of Nicolai and the Scottish lady, related in a former part of this work. The celebrated Dr Samuel Johnson, was prone to superstition, and occasionally afflicted with paroxysms of hypochondriacal illusions. He relates, that as he was one day at Oxford, turning the key of his chamber, he heard his mother (who was at Litchfield) distinctly calling 'Sam.' From which he had wrought up his mind to expect the most woful tidings of his beloved parent, but was entirely and happily disappointed.

Let our youth be taught that the whole phalanx of ghosts, apparitions, witches and wizards, charms and enchantments, second sight, omens and auguries, astrology and fortune telling, vulgar miracles, and vulgar prophecies, should be classed with other vulgarisms, the legitimate offspring of perverted imaginations, and ought to be reprobated as degrading to the human understanding. Those who disdain to believe in their existence, will never be molested by them. 'Resist the devil and he will flee from you.' Firmly resist a belief in witchcraft, and you may bid defiance to all the witches that ever traversed the air or haunted a dwelling.

Strongly impress on the minds of our youth, that superstition and bigotry are derogatory to the cause of genuine religion, giving countenance to inadequate conceptions of the deity, illiberality, and uncharitableness, religious frenzy, tumultuous excitements, fanatical disquietudes, unreal or doubtful conversions, melancholy, gloom, and despair. These evil results are diametrically opposed to that honorable and happy character which the christian religion is so admirably calculated to form and sustain.

We may confer great benefit on our youth, by directing them to a proper course of reading. In a library, without advice, they are in the condition of a stranger in a city without a guide. The world is almost inundated with books; a choice may be made to answer every requirement and to suit every genius and taste.

Popular education has now become almost universally a darling pursuit. Seminaries of learning and improved school institutions, are extending more and more, and will soon be diffused throughout the land, and their benefits equally enjoyed by all classes of our youth. Numerous Lyceums have, within these last few years, been established in New England, and the public voice bespeaks an abundant increase in their numbers; they abound in the best means to excite emulation and diffuse general knowledge. It is auspicious to the public welfare when our citizens are wise, and sober minded, patriotic, chaste, and virtuous, appreciating the free institutions of our fathers, as rich boons from heaven, and the freedom of mind as of inestimable value. The avenues which lead to the fountains of honor and intelligence are as wide and easy of access as those which overwhelm in vice and misery, and those who prefer the former need not pass through life unacquainted with the mighty wonders which the world contains.

It is with regret, that, in 'A Dictionary of important names, objects, and terms found in the holy Scriptures, intended principally for youth,' recently published by Howard Malcolm, A. M., the following definition is found.

'Witch is a woman and Wizard is a man that is supposed to have dealings with Satan, if not actually entered into formal compact with him. That such persons are among men is abundantly plain from Scripture; and that they ought to be put to death.'

It can scarcely be believed that this can be intended as an item in the code of instruction for the rising generation in the 19th century. Our children, it is presumed, have, in these enlightened times, been taught lessons better calculated to instil into their tender minds the principles of moral wisdom and philanthropy. The author has not favored the public with the rules and signs by which witches and wizards are to be designated, and the evidence by which they are to be convicted. Had he lived in witch-hanging times, he might have witnessed with what sang-froid ghosts and spectres could consign witches and wizards to the gallows. Has the author been so fortunate as to ascertain whether the sin of witchcraft, as understood in modern times, is actually denounced as punishable in the holy Scriptures?

In all countries, improvements in literature and the arts and sciences, have been impeded, not only by superstition and bigotry among the ignorant, but by the absurd edicts of sovereigns and legislators, as if to bid defiance to all the energies of progressive knowledge. In the 16th century, the Emperor Charles V. of Spain, although himself addicted to crimes of the blackest stain, ordered an assembly of divines to deliberate, whether it were lawful in point of conscience to dissect a dead body. During the prevalence of a malignant fever in Barcelona, the court of Madrid wrote the prescription to be used, and by command of his Catholic Majesty, the physicians were ordered to adhere to it in all cases, and forbidden to prescribe any other remedy.

In the days of bitter intolerance, Servetus, a learned Spanish physician, discovered the course of the blood through the lungs, called the lesser circulation; and was afterwards cruelly burnt at the stake, with his books, in consequence of a religious controversy with John Calvin.

The immortal Harvey, who, in 1628, was the author of the most important discovery recorded in medical history, the circulation of the blood, was subjected to base calumny and detraction, while bestowing blessings on the world, by his noble efforts and pious example. 'It was, I believe,' says

Lady Morgan, 'late in the last century, that Baron de Luch was executed at Turin, for having published that the earth moves round the sun.' The Chevalier La Barre, a minor, was executed in France for an imputed insult offered to the crucifix.

But, God be praised, the rack of torture and the lighted fagot never have disgraced our native country; nor are these horrid engines any longer in requisition to punish imaginary crimes and to repress truth and philosophical research.

A pious friend and patron of the present writer, dying in the year 1787, without heirs, bequeathed by will his whole estate, except some legacies, to thirteen Congregational Societies in the county in which he lived; the interest of which was to be appropriated, annually, for one hundred years, to the purchase of certain specified religious books, to be distributed among the said Societies. After the expiration of one hundred years, other religious books might be selected by the existing ministers, except, that one year in every four, the books first mentioned only should be purchased. In less than twenty years, the specified books becoming obsolete, new editions were required to be printed for that particular purpose only, which occasioned great expense. The Societies interested became dissatisfied with their restriction to books which were constantly superseded by more recent publications, keeping pace with progressive improvement. They all united in a petition to the legislature that the will might be abolished, which was granted, and the estate sold and the proceeds divided among the several Societies concerned.

Change and decay are stamped in indelible characters upon the proudest productions of man; all bequests on illiberal conditions and human creeds to which men may cling as infallible, can be considered as commensurate only with all earthly objects based on no permanent foundation.

MEDICAL QUACKERY

There may be no impropriety in adding a few pages on the subject of Medical Quackery and empiricism, since, for more than half a century, the writer has occasionally witnessed melancholy scenes and disasters among his fellow-men in consequence of their nefarious practice. It is a matter of congratulation, that from the liberal and excellent provisions made by our legislatures, and the most ample means of education which our institutions afford, every candidate for medical fame may become completely qualified for its attainment. And every town or parish may be supplied with scientific physicians, meriting the confidence of the people; and no other should ever be employed or encouraged, as they have peculiar claim to public patronage.

Notwithstanding that in all the medical institutions in the United States, the most judicious and energetic measures have been adopted to prevent the evils of quackery, there are ignorant and unprincipled impostors, who set at defiance all learning and theoretical knowledge, and practise the vilest acts and deceptions, sporting with the health and lives of their fellow-men without remorse. Such miscreants are too frequently encouraged by the heedless multitude, who, delighting in marvellous and magical airs, readily yield themselves dupes to the grossest absurdities. From one of this character we have the following anecdote.

An old acquaintance who knew well the character of a celebrated empiric, said to him, while standing at the door, 'Prithee, doctor, how is it that you, whose origin I so well know, should have been able to obtain more practice than almost all the regular bred physicians.' 'Pray,' says the quack, 'how many persons have passed us while you put the question?' 'About twenty.' 'And pray how many of them do you suppose possess a competent share of common sense?' 'Perhaps one out of the twenty.' 'Just so,' says the doctor, 'and that one applies to the regular physician, while I and my brethren pick up the other nineteen.'

And how often have we seen the contemptible ignoramus raised by the voice of popularity above the level of the learned and accomplished physician, and boasting of nineteen twentieths of the practice? It is not unfrequent that our attention is arrested by the pretensions of prophets and mystical fanatics, who announce their pretended heavenly mission, and treat their credulous patients with bubbles and magical spells. The stranger, called the rainwater doctor, after gulling hundreds of people of weak minds a few years since, disappeared, leaving both his origin and his exit involved in mystery. But the most audacious impostor that was ever suffered to delude even the vulgar, was one Austin, of Vermont, who, a few years since, proclaimed himself a prophet, and pretended to cure all diseases by prayer to heaven, requiring no other information relative to the patient, than a few lines requesting his prayers. Such was the credulity and such the faith of the multitude, that letters and messengers were despatched to him from the sick, the blind, and the crippled, from the distance of several hundred miles, until thousands had accumulated on his hands. A certain poor man whom I knew, became so infatuated with the prophet's proclamation, that, after collecting letters from a number of invalids, of all descriptions, among whom was one totally blind, and having received contributions in money, actually performed a journey of about two hundred miles to receive the benefit of the prophet's prayers. But he soon returned as he went, and gained for his credulous employers and himself no other benefit than a conviction of their folly, and the vile imposition of modern prophets. The two jugglers above mentioned, it is presumed, jeoparded no lives by the use of poisonous materials, as they depended on the operation of the imagination; but there are bolder champions of the craft who can pop you off the stage in a moment. The country is annoyed by a train of unprincipled ignoramuses, without reputation, who are prowling about, brandishing the sure weapons of death, reckless of consequences. But their punishment is reserved to the day of retributive justice. I well recollect the following moral lesson of a pious physician. 'If a patient die through your wilful ignorance, rashness, or careless neglect, his blood will be required at your hands.' How much greater, then, must be the accountability in those who administer the most active and even poisonous materials, without the smallest acquaintance with the human constitution or the nature of the medicine. It is characteristic of these people, to undertake to cure incurables, magnifying a wart to a rose cancer, a simple ulcer to a spreading mortification, and to set bones where there is neither joint nor fracture. Although palpable instances of death from their practice are frequent, should a single cure happen, it is proclaimed as almost miraculous, and the lawless miscreants are still suffered to seek their prey with impunity, and no one tells of their thousand victims concealed in the silent grave!

It is from a similar empirical source, that the public is annoyed by a disgusting display of quack and patent medicines; which, through the medium of newspapers, are impudently palmed upon public attention. It would seem as though a host of ignorant impostors have leagued in hostility against the profession of medicine, wishing to despoil it of its dignity and usefulness, and prostrate its character in the dust. The world is inundated with nostrums, usurping the power, not only to remedy all the diseases of our nature, but actually to fortify the human constitution, and render it invulnerable. In their ostentatious display, they extol a single nostrum as adequate to the prevention and cure of a whole catalogue of diseases, however opposite or discordant in their nature. They are suited to all constitutions, as the shoe-black's composition is applicable to every one's boots or shoes. Thus are we kindly invited, at the expense of a few dollars, to purchase of those self 'dubbed doctors,' that health and longevity which even the judicious hand of science is unable to bestow. The inventors and venders of these pretended specifics, in most instances, have no knowledge of the diseases which they pretend to cure; they depend, as it were, on a random shot, and whatever may be the issue, they are sure of their enormous gains, from two to four hundred per cent; articles sold for a dollar might be afforded for ten cents.

By such fraud and imposition, a noted Charlatan in London accumulated such an immense fortune as to parade the streets in a splendid equipage, the effects of public credulity. But the public may be assured, that since the great improvements in chemical science, a large proportion of patent medicines have been analyzed, and are found to consist of old articles which physicians have expunged from their materia medica, to give place to more valuable and efficacious remedies. Here, then, is a boundless source of knavery and fraud,--but I desire to have it understood, that these observations are not to extend to all patentees of medical compositions, without exception, for all are not equally censurable. Few, indeed, there are, which scientific physicians are willing to concede may be of public utility. But that indiscriminate application in all cases and circumstances, should be most pointedly reprobated. Were the annual amount of money expended for useless nostrums made public, it would excite astonishment, and were the innumerable disappointments in their creative powers promulgated, public indignation and contempt would be the portion of the inventors and venders of patented nostrums.

There is not a more provoking absurdity, as applied to the economy of health, than the idea of spring medicines, family medicines, &c, and it should be distinctly understood by every individual, that such medicine administered to persons in health, as preventive of disease, as well as those administered without a skilful reference to the present condition of the system, are absolutely dangerous to health and life. And the same observation will apply to the practice of blood-letting in the spring season.

Those who maintain the ridiculous idea that individuals are endowed with supernatural gifts and knowledge, and become skilful physicians without education or study, betray a pitiful credulity, equalled only by the conceits of those who believe in ghosts and spectres, haunting the dwellings of the dead. We now witness with the deepest interest, the rapid strides in the march of intellect, keeping pace with the advance of light and truth, looking for that political and moral millenium, when knowledge will be more sought for than wealth, and the charms of virtue more prized than those of vice; when prejudice, superstition, and licentiousness, will be discountenanced among all classes of mankind, and righteousness shall exalt our nation.

Truly 'the lines have fallen to us in pleasant places, and we have a goodly heritage.' But it were unjust to look back to antiquity and compare the beauties of the present day with the deformities of ancient times; to attribute exclusive perfection to ourselves and deprive our ancestors of their real worth and merit; for we know not the period among them when wisdom and virtue were lightly esteemed. Let us reflect, with religious gratitude, on the momentous privileges and benefits bequeathed to us by our fathers. In all their actions we trace a zealous solicitude to transmit to posterity a glorious inheritance. Like angels of light, they would illuminate the minds of their children, with the high importance of religious institutions, seminaries, and free schools. If, in any form, they would enchain our minds, it would be in the principles of civil and religious freedom, of patriotism, philanthropy, moral rectitude, and public virtue. But 'our fathers, where are they?' Let us with laborious fidelity follow them in every good word and work, that our children may, in the spirit of gratitude and love, reiterate the exclamation 'our fathers, where are they?' It is our glorious privilege to live in an age when the elements of our terrestrial abode are rendered subservient to the most stupendous operations. The works of men's hands appear as if endowed with intelligence; the heated steam subverts the power of the fleetest steed, and the facilities of traversing the earth and seas, are like the airy flights of the feathered tribe. But oh! humbling consideration, death triumphs over the frail nature of man; our life is but a continued miracle, capable of being sustained only by the hand of that omnipotent being whom we adore as the 'former of our bodies, and the father of our spirits.' All must bow to the awful summons, and quit this earthly tabernacle; the last remains of mortality are consigned to the silent tomb to mingle with the parent dust.

www.ingramcontent.com/pod-product-compliance
Lightning Source LLC
Chambersburg PA
CBHW071916070526
44583CB00016B/2015